Ron Beiswenger

Western
Water
Made
Simple

High Country News

Western Water Made Simple

ISLAND PRESS

Washington, D.C. □ *Covelo, California*

About Island Press

Island Press, a nonprofit organization, publishes, markets, and distributes the most advanced thinking on the conservation of our natural resources — books about soil, land, water, forests, wildlife, and hazardous and toxic wastes. These books are practical tools used by public officials, business and industry leaders, natural resource managers, and concerned citizens working to solve both local and global resource problems.

Founded in 1978, Island Press reorganized in 1984 to meet the increasing demand for substantive books on all resource-related issues. Island Press publishes and distributes under its own imprint and offers these services to other nonprofit organizations.

Funding to support Island Press is provided by Mary Reynolds Babcock Foundation, The Ford Foundation, the George Gund Foundation, the William and Flora Hewlett Foundation, The Joyce Foundation, The Andrew W. Mellon Foundation, Northwest Area Foundation, The J.N. Pew, Jr. Charitable Trust, Rockefeller Brothers Fund, and The Tides Foundation.

For additional information about Island Press publishing services and a catalog of current and forthcoming titles, contact Island Press, P.O. Box 7, Covelo, California 95428.

© 1987 High Country News

This Island Press volume is the first book edition of four special issues of *High Country News* that were originally published in the late fall of 1986. This volume includes some updating and minor revision of the newspaper issues.

Cover design by Lester Doré

Library of Congress Cataloging-in-Publication Data

Western water made simple.

"Contains the contents of four special issues
of High Country News from the fall of 1986" —
Pref.
  Bibliography: p. 217
  Includes index.
  1. Water-supply — West (U.S.) 2. Water-supply —
Missouri River Watershed. 3. Water-supply — Colorado
River Watershed (Colo.-Mexico) 4. Water-supply —
Columbia River Watershed. I. Marston, Ed. II. High Country News
TD223.6.W48   1987   333.91'00978   87–17222
ISBN 0–933280–39–4

MANUFACTURED IN THE UNITED STATES OF AMERICA

Contents

Part Three

The Missouri River: In Search of Destiny

Part Four

The Colorado River As Plumbing

Preface

I f you ever skied with an eight-year-old, you have some sense of
this book and of the newspaper that created it. An eight-year-old
skis close to the ground, goes in and out of a snowplow, and
tackles slopes more skilled adult skiers avoid.

High Country News is that youngster—it sticks close to the
ground, moves mostly in an inelegant crouch, and often ends up in
territory shunned by older, larger, more elegant colleagues.

This book, which contains the contents of four special issues of
High Country News from the fall of 1986, illustrates the above
characteristics. The special issues were about the massive and intimidating subject of Western water. Books have been written about one
stream, about one piece of water legislation, about one ditch. It is
rumored that there isn't enough water in the entire West, even in a wet
year, to drown all of the region's water experts or to float to the oceans
all of the legal briefs that have been filed in Western water courts.

The most any newspaper—especially one whose home is a remote
coal-mining and fruit-growing Colorado town of 1400—could rea-
sonably attempt would be to take one small piece of the vast Western
water story and tell it in some detail.

Instead, *HCN* took as the scope of its special issues the three
major Western river basins: the Colorado, the Columbia, and the
Missouri. To make matters worse, it failed to pay obeisance to the
intimidating nature of its material, as the collective title *Western
Water Made Simple* demonstrates. Eight-year-old skiers, you see,
don't stand up often enough, or tall enough, to be frightened by the
heights below them.

The crouching, snowplow approach to water was well received.
Demand far outstripped supply for the first three issues. It took until

the fourth issue for the newspaper's staff to realize it was making a good run down the slopes and to drastically increase the number of copies being printed.

In addition, the four issues caught the eyes of nominators and judges in the humid East, and the paper received the 1986 George Polk Award for Environmental Reporting. (Among the winners in the other 11 categories were *The New York Times, Newsweek,* and "CBS Reports.")

As a result of both the unfilled demand for copies and complaints from readers that an unindexed set of four newspapers was difficult to store and refer to, Island Press decided to issue *Western Water Made Simple* as a book.

It is said that there is nothing so dated as yesterday's newspaper, and the contents of the four issues are undoubtedly aging even as you skim this preface.

But the major themes of the book — that Western water can, and must, be understood by the nonspecialist; that the Columbia River is in an age of reform; that the Missouri River and the land it drains are in limbo; and that the Colorado River can best be understood as plumbing — are true today and will be true for many years.

The staff of *High Country News* tried in the newspaper version of *Western Water Made Simple* to thank those who made the water issues possible. We are not going to repeat those thanks here, except in two special cases. First, we thank the generations of readers, writers, and staff who somehow have kept the small, unlikely, fortnightly newspaper alive for 17 years. Second, we thank the 777 Fund of the Tides Foundation in San Francisco for the grant that paid for the writing, production, and distribution of *Western Water Made Simple* in newspaper form.

Ed Marston, Publisher
For the staff of
High Country News

Contributors

Marjane Ambler is a freelance writer who specializes in Indian issues, and a former editor of *High Country News*. She currently lives in Yellowstone National Park.

Allen Best is a reporter for the *Vail Trail* in Vail, Colorado. He formerly edited newspapers at Winter Park and Dremmling, Colorado.

Peter Carrels is a freelance writer who lives in Aberdeen, South Dakota.

Daniel Keith Conner does full-time research at the Sea Grant Legal Program at the University of Mississippi. He has both a law degree and training in oceanography.

Lester Doré is an artist and conservationist. He lives in the Ocooch Mountains of southwestern Wisconsin.

Pat Ford is a freelance writer and conservationist in Boise, Idaho. He directed the Idaho Conservation League for several years.

Bob Gottlieb and **Peter Wiley** are California writers whose syndicated column is published by newspapers around the nation. They are also authors of several books, including *America's Saints: The Rise of Mormon Power.*

Rose Houk is a freelance writer and editor who specializes in natural resource topics. She lives in Grand Junction, Colorado.

Verne Huser is a program associate in Sante Fe, New Mexico, with Western Network, a nonprofit research and mediation organization that specializes in natural resources.

Paul Krza lives in Rock Springs, Wyoming, where he is the southwest Wyoming regional correspondent for the Casper *Star-Tribune*. He pays special attention to the U.S. Bureau of Reclamation.

Betsy Marston has been editor of *High Country News* in Paonia, Colorado, since 1983.

Ed Marston has been publisher of *High Country News* in Paonia, Colorado, since 1983.

Mary Moran, a geologist, was a staff member of *High Country News* from 1983 until early 1986. She was a research associate on Western Water Made Simple. She now lives in Tucson, Arizona.

Lawrence Mosher is a journalist in Washington, D.C. He has written for *National Geographic* and *National Journal,* and now publishes a newsletter called *The Water Reporter.*

Ed Quillen is a freelance writer, weekly columnist for the *Denver Post*, and resident of Salida, Colorado.

C. L. Rawlins is *High Country News'* poetry editor. He has also worked on acid deposition studies in Wyoming's Bridger Wilderness since 1985. He lives in Boulder, Wyoming.

Hadley Roberts is a retired U.S. Forest Service wildlife biologist living in Salmon, Idaho. He currently works as a wildlife consultant and big game guide.

Cynthia D. Stowell is a writer and photographer based in Portland, Oregon. *Faces of a Reservation,* about the people of the Warm Springs Reservation, is due out in 1987.

Douglas Towne is a geographer who studied the relationship of irrigation decline to landscape at the University of Arizona. He currently lives in Denver, Colorado.

José Trava is a soil scientist who worked in the Mexicali Valley of Mexico, and who now works in Mexico City. He is associated with the Institute of the NorthAmerican West.

Peter Wild is a professor of English at the University of Arizona, and writes for numerous publications on the West in general and water in particular.

Charles Wilkinson is professor of law at the University of Colorado, an authority on Indian and Western resources law, and a widely published author. *The Lords of Yesterday,* an account of how 19th century resource laws affect today's decisions, is due out shortly.

Chuck Williams is author-photographer of *Bridge of the Gods, Mountains of Fire*, a history of the Columbia Gorge. He is also author of several other books and articles, and did investigative journalism for Friends of the Earth. Williams, who is part Cascade Indian, edits *CRITFC News* for the Columbia River Inter-Tribal Fish Commission.

David Wilson is an artist and illustrator who lives in Durango, Colorado.

Part One

Western Water Made Simple

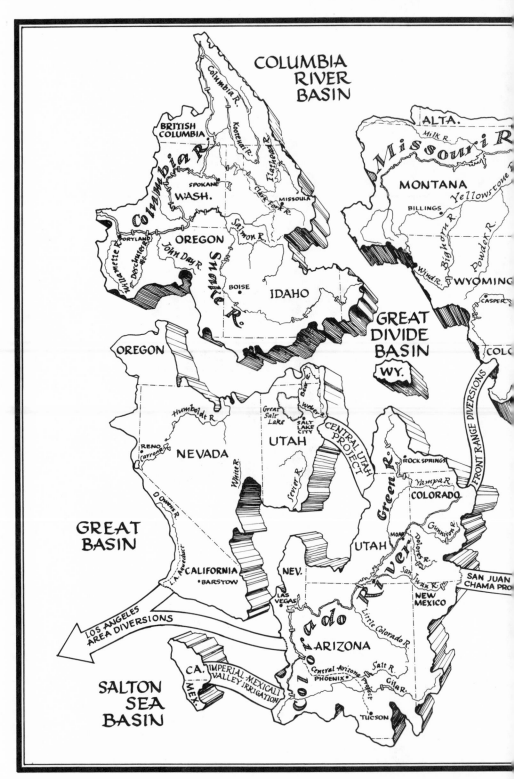

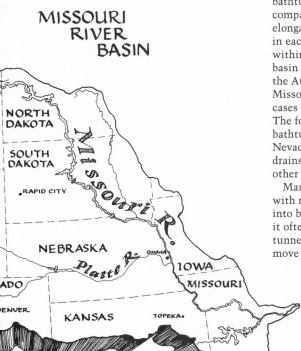

MISSOURI RIVER BASIN

NORTH DAKOTA

SOUTH DAKOTA

•RAPID CITY

NEBRASKA

Platte R. OMAHA•

IOWA

ADO

MISSOURI

DENVER•

KANSAS

TOPEKA•

COLORADO RIVER BASIN

MAP COMPILED AND EDITED BY MARY MORAN
RENDERED BY LESTER DORÉ

The West is composed of four major bathtubs. Three are river basin bathtubs: the sprawling Missouri, the compact Columbia, and the elongated Colorado. The major river in each basin collects water that falls within the natural boundaries of that basin and dumps it, eventually, into the Atlantic, in the case of the Missouri, and into the Pacific, in the cases of the Columbia and Colorado. The fourth of the West's major bathtubs, the Great Basin of Utah and Nevada, has no outlet. Its water drains into the Great Salt Lake and other closed sinks, and stays there.

Man has not been willing to live with nature's division of the West into basins. So, when it suits us, and it often suits us, we build canals, tunnels and pumping stations to move water from one basin to another. The San Juan-Chama diversion puts Colorado River water in the Rio Grande basin, and thence on to the Gulf of Mexico. Denver's Front Range captures water out of the Colorado River basin and sends it under the Continental Divide, into the Missouri. On the other side of the Colorado River basin, the Central Utah Project transfers water from the Colorado to the Great Basin. Southern California, the greatest diverter of all time, pulls water out of many places, including the Owens River (of *Chinatown* fame) in the Great Basin and the Colorado River. The desert irrigators on the California-Mexico border transfer Colorado River water into the closed Salton Sea basin. The megalopolis around Los Angeles dumps its water into the Pacific Ocean.

	COLUMBIA RIVER BASIN	MISSOURI RIVER BASIN	COLORADO RIVER BASIN
River length (miles)	1,214	2,315	1,450
Basin size (square miles)	258,500	530,000	235,000
Average annual runoff (acre-feet)	182.5 million 180–185 m	61.5 million	15 million
Average flow at river mouth (acre-feet)	185 million	52	0
Irrigated land (acres)	7.0 million	14.1 million	2.2 million
Reservoir storage — active capacity (acre-feet)	41 million	75 million	58.9 million
Hydropower Capacity (megawatts)	22,000	3,300	3,786

It is said that if you ask 40 million Frenchmen a question, you will get 40 million different answers. The same thing can be said of those who tabulate information on rivers. The numbers in the table were compiled from a variety of sources and reconciled to the extent possible. But they should be treated as approximations rather than absolute truth.

1

The West's Water-crats and Dam-icans

Ed Marston

From the end of the Civil War to the 1960s, the South was dominated by the politics of race. The singlemindedness of the South gave the region great influence in the U.S. Congress. It was, however, the influence of negation and inflexibility. The South spent its national political capital making the sun stand still, even as it kept its own society rigid in the armor of a segregated, unequal society.

It was not until the region's politics of race shattered that the South could advance. A society of lords and serfs is not vital, creative, or productive, and the South could not take its place among other regions until the old order crumbled.

The West also comes close to practicing single-issue politics – in its case, the politics of water. The South had its Dixiecrats; the West has its Water-crats and Dam-icans. The South spent its political capital stopping bills that would have given blacks opportunity. The West spends its political capital pushing the Central Arizona Project, the Central Utah Project, the Columbia Basin expansion, the Garrison Diversion, Animas-LaPlata and a flood of smaller projects.

The South was organized, from the courthouse up, to guarantee that those who might favor a more open society never came near power. Anyone running for public office faced a series of tough loyalty

Mike McClure

tests on race. So eminent a figure as former Arkansas Senator J.W. Fulbright, fearless though he was on foreign affairs, toed the line on race.

Similarly, Western politicians often earn the freedom to be open on other issues by being hardnosed on water development. Senator Gary Hart voted for every Colorado water project. When he was governor, Ed Herschler helped ensure that Wyoming's uranium-oil-gas-coal boom didn't bury the state in debris. But on water he was the dam-builders' Robin Hood, proposing the diversion of $600 million of Wyoming's mineral wealth to state-built dams and canals.

Arizona Congressman Morris Udall is a strong conservationist, but he is even stronger when it comes to water projects — especially the multibillion-dollar Central Arizona Project. That project has shaped Arizona's politics since statehood in 1912, when Arizona sent Carl Hayden to the U.S. Congress. There he began an effort that culminated in 1968 with the authorization of the Central Arizona Project. In 1969, his 56-year-long job done, 92-year-old Hayden left the Senate.

Hayden is an extreme, but not unique, example. Western Colorado's long-time Congressman Wayne Aspinall spent his career shepherding the water projects through Congress by crafting arrangements among the Western states. Aspinall's power rested on a rural home district where political power lay in part with water conservancy districts. These districts are taxing entities whose boards are appointed by judges, since water is too important in the West to be left to the vagaries of elections. The districts' mission is to use their taxing power to raise seed money to convince the federal government to build the locals a water project.

Conservancy districts are the political base on which much of the rural West rests, and they have proven stable, long-lived and potent. The ranchers and farmers who man the districts' boards and who stand to benefit from the federally financed water projects are leaders in their communities. Until recently, they and their fellow farmers and ranchers weren't blown away by busts, the way miners and loggers were.

Part of their invincibility rested on a way of life that is both admirable and stable. The Rocky Mountain cow-calf operation is the ideal economic unit for a vigorous, intelligent, self-reliant family. With some exceptions, the cow-calf men have dominated the rural Rocky Mountain state legislature and congressional delegations. In theory, the U.S. Supreme Court's one man, one-vote edict also applies to the West. In practice, a rancher's political influence is roughly one hundred times greater than that of a non-rancher in the West.

In part, the ranchers have earned that clout through a creative, tenacious form of land-development. The cow-calf operation has evolved over the past century into a close fit with the mountain geography and political landscape. At the center of the ideal operation is a homeplace — flat meadowlands below 7,500 feet or so, irrigated each summer by the snowmelt coming off nearby mountains. Attached to the homeplace are high country grazing leases granted by the Forest Service essentially in perpetuity, and as much a property right as the private land itself.

The cows and their spring calves spend June through September grazing on the national forest land, moving upward in search of new grass as the snow melts. With the cows and calves more or less minding themselves, the ranch family is free to spend the summer irrigating fields and harvesting one or two cuttings of hay.

When the herd returns from the hills in the fall a step ahead of the hunting season, the calf crop is sold to a feedlot and mother cows are fed on the hay during the winter. In March, a new crop of calves hits the ground, and the cycle begins again.

Winter or summer, the operation provides vigorous, varied outdoor work. The Western rancher is part farmer, part cowboy, part entrepreneur, working year-round surrounded by the most beautiful landscape on earth. The kind of work and the landscape helps explain why so many urbanites yearn to own a ranch.

The irrigation water used to raise the hay those mother cows chomp on all winter usually flows out of a federally built water project. That means the water is practically free to the rancher; the cost is subsidized by everyone from the national taxpayer to the people who use the electricity produced by the West's network of dams. For good measure, the cows and calves graze all summer on land the rancher essentially owns on long-term leases from the Forest Service or Bureau of Land Management. Like the water, the cost of these grazing leases is a bargain.

The land shapes the rancher as much as his irrigation systems shape it. Unlike the dryland farmer or the 19th century cowboy, the cow-calf rancher must be a social, political creature. He either cooperates by joining together to get the U.S. Bureau of Reclamation to build a project and then to keep that project's dams and canals maintained, or he and his enterprise die.

The cowboy, or rather the rancher-farmer, has been incredibly successful in establishing an economy and way of life that has dominated the rural West for almost a century in some of the most difficult country in the United States. Drive into any remote mountain valley, climb steep trails toward almost any mountain pass, wander across any parched BLM acreage or up any wash in southern Utah, and you will find the land marked by dams and ditches or by cows munching on the federal grass.

You have to love cattle to think they do the high country much good. But in the valleys, on the irrigated homeplaces, the cow-calf man has created a beautiful landscape. The green hayfields, bordered by unobtrusive irrigation ditches and surrounded by sage desert, present a varied appearance from their first greening up in the spring through the appearance of windrows and bales.

The physical altering and occupation of the land is accomplished by a social and political presence. Based on their land use, the ranchers have created the ideal environment for families and small rural

David Spear

communities. It is ideal because the need to build and maintain the irrigation system (maintaining ditches in mountainous, unstable country can be as hard as building them) enforces cooperation and contacts to the outside world.

But the largest effect of ranchers on the West goes beyond the unique landscape or the communities built on that landscape. Their lasting effect is the Western worldview they have created and then lent, or rather given, to the region's extractive industries.

The worldview is that of a fiercely independent rural people who insist, as their right, that government do everything it can to support their independent way of life. Examples abound showing how that world has spread beyond irrigation systems and cattle. But let us take nuclear power, just because it seems to be so remote from a rancher raising hay in Montana's Bitterroot Valley.

Congressman Wayne Aspinall was best known for his work on water. But he was also dominant on the joint House-Senate committee on atomic energy, where he worked to protect the nuclear industry from "overregulation" and to channel federal subsidies to it. There was a clear connection between his water and nuclear activities. Just as the West had arid land that needed water, so it had huge amounts of uranium, most of which was beneath public land. A thriving, subsidized nuclear energy industry was essential to the West's uranium industry.

The West would not have been successful with the federal treasury had it felt it was asking for handouts. But it never saw itself as a beggar. Instead, it saw itself the way a Pentagon general sees himself when he comes to Congress for weapons money.

The rural Western ethic is that all wealth comes out of the ground, either as grass growing or as minerals being mined. The butchering and marketing of the animals raised on the grass, the smelting and shaping of the mined ore into pitchforks or pins or computer parts, are all very well. But these are derivative, second-class activities, only possible because farmers and ranchers and miners and loggers have provided the stuff of wealth.

This economic vision of the world helps explain why ranchers and farmers are reluctant to market their product. It is as if knights were to demean themselves by plowing land they had conquered. It is why in the West the agricultural community has almost always formed coalitions with the extractive industries, and opposed the environmental movement. Why the phrase "tourist industry" seems as laughable to a farmer or rancher as the idea of a "service industry."

Urbanites tend to see farmers and ranchers as hardworking and productive, but also as naive people in need of protection from the realities of the world. As a result they acquiesce, often good-naturedly, to farm programs that would enrage them if they were directed at insurance companies or automakers. It would be interesting to see if that attitude could survive exposure to what traditional ranchers and farmers believe — that people in factories and offices and barberships are doing work that, if not useless and foolish, is certainly far down on any scale they can think of.

So the fact that today's reclamation projects — such as Garrison, CUP, Animas-LaPlata — cost a few million dollars for each farmer they put on the land, doesn't cause their proponents to blink. That, they say, is the price society pays for creating the stuff of wealth. Without it and the other industries based on the earth, there is nothing.

It was this ethic that led to the damming of the Columbia River in the Northwest so that the once mighty river is now nothing but a series of lakes, with the tail of one backed up against the dam above it. It is why the Colorado River in most years no longer reaches the Pacific, instead dying an arid, salty death in the deserts of northern Mexico. It is why both the Columbia and Colorado are more plumbing than river. Almost any stretch of either river can be turned on or off by the flick of a switch.

It is why the Missouri is dammed to within an inch of no longer being a river in its upper basin states. The plains of Montana, North

Dakota and South Dakota are occupied by the sprawling Pick-Sloan reservoirs; they provide hydroelectric power, flood control, and navigation water for the humid states below, while the lower Missouri, thanks to the Army Corps of Engineers, is more channel than river.

But in each of the three river basins, there are signs that an era has come to an end. The major sign comes from the U.S. Congress. Just as an earlier Congress told the South through the Civil Rights Act of 1964 that an era had ended, so have the last several Congresses told the West, by not voting funds for new water projects, that the water project era has ended.

As protracted and noisy as an operatic death, that ending has caused screams of anguish and outrage. The Dakotas say they were doublecrossed. They lost enormous amounts of river-bottom land to Pick-Sloan reservoirs, but did not get the irrigation projects that were to make up for the losses.

The upper Colorado River basin states, especially Colorado, charge that the U.S. Congress has deprived them of water that was their birthright, while giving California and Arizona all the development funds they can spend.

Pressure for change has come not just from the U.S. Congress. In the decades following World War II, the Northwest states grew addicted to the cheap hydropower generated by the dammed Columbia. When there were no more rivers to dam, the region undertook to build the five giant Washington Public Power Supply System nuclear power plants, following the public-private partnership approach that had built the region's dams and irrigation projects. The resulting debacle helped lead the Columbia River basin into an age of reform centered on the recovery of that region's salmon fishery.

Just as the drive to harness rivers led to a political and economic model that favored other extractive industries, so the present effort to recover the salmon fishery has led to a model that encouraged other forms of conservation. The reform push has led to the bypassing of hydroelectric generators to save fish, to the curtailing of logging to reduce sediment that would destroy spawning beds, to the modifying of irrigation projects to prevent salmon from ending up flopping amidst irrigated fruit trees and cornfields, to a new emphasis on water quality. It is as if the Northwest hit a brick wall, and bounced away heading in a totally new direction.

The situation is more subtle on the Colorado River. That basin is as plumbed as the Columbia. There are tunnels and pumps to carry its water into the Great Salt Lake basin of Utah, into the Missouri River basin of the Colorado Front Range and thence on to the Mississippi, to southern California outside of the basin, and to Phoenix and Tucson, within it.

A small fraction of the Colorado River's water is used for cities and industry. Most of it irrigates crops — mainly hay for cattle — and generates electricity. Informally, the river's urban, electric, and agricultural users may accommodate wildlife and recreation. They leave reservoirs high into the fall, if possible, and try to keep a trickle in a stream to support fish.

But that is *noblesse oblige,* and only to be counted on until the water is needed on the land. For the basis of Western water law is the dewatering of every stream and river in the region. Water in streams has no rights. Even where in-stream and minimum stream flow laws exist, they have marginal effects. The rafting industry is far better off today than it would be without dams. But it exists at the whim of users who are interested in irrigation, hydropower, and municipal and industrial uses.

So while the Columbia is firmly embarked on an era of reform, the Colorado is in an ambiguous position. There are no salmon on the Colorado to bind the river system together. Its own endangered species — the humpbacked chub and the squawfish — do not have the Indian-sportsmen-commercial fishery constituency the salmon has.

Pressure on the Colorado River comes from other directions. First, the extractive economies, including the cow-calf operations, are dying. That's the stick of change. The carrot is the increasing value of water for urban and recreation uses.

San Diego and other southern California cities, as well as Phoenix and Tucson, say they desperately need water. Within the Rockies, the recreation industry says it could rescue Colorado, Idaho, and western Montana if it had the water to work with. Numbers show that even though they must piggyback on other water uses, rafting, fishing, hunting, hiking, and sightseeing generate amounts of money that are in the same ballpark as agriculture, logging or mining. But these recreation and lifestyle uses all depend on water — water in streams, in full reservoirs, and in shallow aquifers to maintain wetlands and marshes.

The title of this book is *Western Water Made Simple,* and the title is certainly a sign of the times. Until this decade, Western water had grown increasingly ornate, adorned by layer on layer of regulation, law, and precedent. Ministering to that body of legal doctrine and practice were the conservancy districts, their attorneys, the state engineers, the elected officials.

Even harsh critics of the water system had to be canonical — had to speak in the liturgy of the established church. Their criticism came through only in the way in which they used the liturgy, much as a secret atheist might wonder aloud in Sunday school: Now just where did Cain's wife come from, anyway?

Jane Coumantaros

Water was complex for the same reason that Louis XIV's government was complex. It was hedged round by moats and walls meant to separate it from outside forces; meant to make it as self-sufficient, as unchanging as possible. Until recently, if you wanted to know about Western water, you had to learn about the Colorado River Compact of 1922, about *Arizona versus California*, about the doctrines of prior appropriation and beneficial use, about senior and junior rights, about first in time and first in right, about the history of Pick-Sloan, about "water is for fighting and liquor is for drinking."

Those embellishments won't disappear. But it is possible today to speak of making Western water simple because it is becoming naked to the world. It no longer exists in an armored cocoon of congressional appropriations, judicially appointed water conservancy districts, and a conservative, landed, rural class.

For better or worse, water is becoming a commodity. Until now, Western water was mostly tied to the land, which meant it was tied to agriculture. It was not subject to trade for dollars. Several years ago, Wyoming was told that tens of millions of dollars could be saved by retiring land in central Wyoming instead of building facilities to remove the salt that farming put into the water. It seemed logical to retire the land. But Wyoming said that the Big Sandy Project must stay in production, and it has, to the best of its marginal ability. Wyoming reacted much as the Catholic Church would were it told that it could make billions by moving the Vatican to make room for a shopping center.

Those traditional attitudes are disappearing in the face of Gramm-Rudman-Hollings, the decline in ranching and mining and logging, and the emergence of economic activities based on water flowing in streams rather than through turbines or over fields.

Western water is becoming simple because it is entering the world in which the rest of us live. It is becoming subject to forces we are all familiar with. After decades of a cloistered existence, it has rejoined the secular, profane, hand-to-mouth world the rest of us are so familiar with.

2

The Corps Adapts, the Bureau Founders

Lawrence Mosher

Hey diddle diddle,
Gramm Rudman's a tickle
Bob Broadbent's flown the coop.
The water babies cried
Over projects denied,
And the Corps run off
with the loot.

If you think the Reagan Revolution stands for preserving traditional Western water interests, think again. The Reagan people
would like to humor those interests, but the new fiscal realities
are undermining their ability to do so. The biggest federal budget
deficit in history is the hammer that is destroying the old order, even
though the environmental era laid the foundation for change.

Western water politics buried Jimmy Carter's second-term hopes
as much as the Ayatollah Khomeini did. Carter's 1977 water project
"hit list" enraged water-users all over the "Reclamation" West. And in
Washington, D.C., his efforts to turn an interdepartmental waif called
the Water Resources Council into a tough water-projects traffic cop

died even before Carter's first term ended, axed to death by peeved congressional budgeteers.

But Carter's vision, without Carter and his council, is firmly on track. And what the Georgian environmentalist couldn't do, federal budget deficits are doing. The Reagan administration is caught in a fiscal vise that is squeezing the federal water agencies dry.

Robert N. Broadbent, who ran the Bureau of Reclamation before becoming an assistant Interior Secretary, has returned to Nevada to run an airport. An excellent administrator and personally popular, he left behind a beleaguered, circle-the-wagons agency dogged by both Gramm-Rudman-Hollings and the ever more obvious perils of desert irrigation.

Over at the Pentagon, the Army Corps of Engineers has proven more flexible. It apparently realizes it must change to survive in these new times. But as the budget-manpower chart shows, in the short run both agencies are hurting.

In the past 10 years, the Corps' construction budget has shrunk 34 percent. Bureau construction has fallen 28 percent. To figure the real drop, add 20 percent for inflation. Manpower has also dwindled. There are 15 percent fewer people at the Corps, and 10 percent fewer at the Bureau.

The Reagan administration's drive to shrink government accounts for some of this reduction. But the major reason is the 10-year moratorium on new water projects. Congress, responding to an alliance of environmentalists and fiscal conservatives, has not approved a major new water work since 1976. In 1984, operations and maintenance spending exceeded construction for the first time in Corps history. But an end to that construction drought seems at hand, in large part due to an internal change at the Corps.

The Corps' Strategy for Survival

One of the quieter shifts to take place since 1980 has occurred at the Corps, where William R. Gianelli, Reagan's first assistant Army Secretary for civil works, lit the fires of cost-sharing. Gianelli, the 'father' of California's water development, realized that unless local interests would pay a significant share of up-front costs, the Corps' construction arm would continue to wither. Robert K. Dawson, who replaced Gianelli three years ago, has picked up the cost-sharing torch.

Although the 40-year-old Dawson is a graduate of the pork-barrel system—he was staff administrator of the House Public Works and Transportation Committee for seven years—his approach has evoked

Robert K. Dawson   Robert K. Broadbent

praise even from such environmental critics as Brent Blackwelder, the Environmental Policy Institute's top water guru:

"Dawson has pursued the cost-sharing initiative with vigor," Blackwelder allows, although he faults the Corps for still promoting 'structural' solutions rather than water conservation and efficiency. Blackwelder likes cost-sharing and user fees, but would also like to see alternatives to dredging, channelizing, and other traditional approaches to water.

On the day in March 1986 that the Senate passed its version of the omnibus water bill, the Corps' Dawson said, "If we are able to devise a new charter or cost-sharing partnership, we're going to have a strong federal water resources program, with the Corps as the largest and pre-eminent participant. But if we don't get a new charter, then I see that program withering away. It just comes down to whether we get this legislation."

In pursuit of the legislation, which became law in November 1986, Dawson convened an unlikely legislative strategy session in his Pentagon quarters the previous July: it pulled in most of the top Washington environmental leaders. Amazingly, Dawson and representatives of the Sierra Club, National Wildlife Federation, Environmental Policy Institute, Wildlife Management Institute, National Audubon Society, Izaak Walton League, and Friends of the Earth came together.

Light at the end of the (water) tunnel

In the spring of 1986, a week before the House of Representatives approved the $902.2 million Garrison Diversion Project in North Dakota, Lawrence Mosher interviewed George Miller, a California Democrat who is chairman of the Interior and Insular Affairs Subcommittee on Water and Power. Excerpts from that interview follow:

Q. What is the future for federal water agencies?

A. They would like to argue that their role has not changed, because they see themselves as very multi-faceted organizations. But the fact is that they have not placed equal emphasis on these facets, but rather a singular emphasis on developmental projects. The other concerns — water conservation, management, new technology — have taken a back seat. But projects are less relevant today than a decade ago. The public understands this, and now the governmental agencies must too.

We have gone through a decade of major transition in which there has been a virtual moratorium on public works projects. Now there is a re-emergence (the water bills) in an entirely new atmosphere and requiring a new coalition. We will be bringing the Garrison project to the floor of the House next week. (The bill passed April 23, 1986: 254 to 154.) To get this bill this far, after a five-year delay, has required a coalition of local input, environmental concern, and the water agencies all on an equal footing now.

If you look at the projects still on the drawing board that would merit consideration by this committee, a very clear message has been sent that if anyone thinks they can just put their head down and ram a project through the Congress of the United States, they will get a big, big headache and no project. Unless you include the environmental community and serious economic studies in lieu of phony feasibility studies, you cannot run that gauntlet now. The beneficiaries are now too small in number compared to the high costs.

Q. How have the congressional dynamics changed?

A. The current legislation is a major test, but let's remember that only three or four years ago people here were saying no way in hell will we ever have cost-sharing. Now we're bargaining over the percentages. Yes, the House Public Works Committee is another scene, but the debate is still different now than only a few years ago. What has happened, driven by the federal deficit, is that Western water development or Mississippi River basin development, or various inland waterway improvements are no longer the sole purview of the members of Congress and senators from that state. Because of the deficit, the community of review now involves many more members of Congress than it did when I came here 12 years ago.

Part of it is a response to something that happened when I first got here, which was that the Interior committee used to be the exclusive jurisdiction of the 17 Western states. Then Congressman Phil Burton started putting Easterners on it. He put people like Phil Sharp of Indiana on it, and all of a sudden members

Richard A. Bloom

California Representative George Miller

started asking questions. Now the barn door is open, and a lot of people are asking questions. And now you have to respond—not like the old days.

Q. What about the Corps of Engineers?

A. I don't think there's any question that the Corps of Engineers is turning around. Their constituency is greater in number than the Bureau of Reclamation, but yes, they are turning around. I sit on the budget committee and I see what drives the process, and we have a number of proposals in the budget committee to start to change the federal-state shares of financing projects.

The rule is that change is incremental. You don't do it in one step. But the whole process now is more accelerated than four or five years ago.

Q. What is the future for irrigated farming in the arid West?

A. Because of Kesterson (the National Wildlife Refuge in California polluted with selenium), we now have to look for drainage problems in a lot of irrigation projects. We are looking at the kinds of lands involved. With the Garrison project, one of the questions we raised was the ability of those lands to absorb irrigation water. There is a great deal of urgency to find out how you contain this problem of drainage pollution.

Q. Should the Corps and Bureau of Reclamation merge?

A. Two bad reputations don't make a saint. I don't think this is terribly relevant. The question is how do you get both of these agencies—it used to be the consensus that the Corps was the worst of the two—to use their talents to deal with today's problems as opposed to the problems they inherited from the 1940s and 1950s. That's the big challenge. If the outside organizations, whether they are environmental, budgetary, scientific, or whatever, are forcing these agencies to do this, and if they don't change, they're going to get left behind.

This is the problem with Kesterson. The Interior Department wants to stumble along with Kesterson and the drainage problem in the valley for another decade, and massage it and look at it and hold conferences. But our committee is rapidly losing its confidence in the Bureau, and is starting to look for alternatives. Perhaps we ought to let the local irrigation districts or local communities deal with this, and if we're culpable in creating the problem, then maybe our role is to finance the solution without dictating it.

We want scientific standards and goals in the cleanup. But we're running out of patience with the Interior Department because its agencies don't have any sense of urgency that toxics dictate you must have today. The science is now showing that the toxics are running a little faster than the bureaucracies. We thought they were isolated in the soils and plant life, and now we see these toxics are moving up the chain. And yet the department has thwarted the one or two efforts out there because they didn't think of them first. And that is not winning any fans in the Congress.

Q. *Is the Kesterson pollution problem causing farmers to consider retiring their land and marketing their water to the cities?*

A. It is stimulating a discussion. But it remains to be seen whether it will result in a development of a water market in California. There are a number of serious questions. The public has an interest: what happens to its share of the water? There are also serious questions about the long-term utilization and management of this resource that have not yet been properly addressed.

There is no question that the problem of drainage at Kesterson has accelerated the discussion. In selected cases water markets will become a reality. In some cases, however, you may not want water markets to develop, because you have the ability in the present system to reallocate water to another use through intentional decisions dictated by market forces.

If you end up with pure water marketing, all the water in the state of California would end up between Santa Barbara and San Diego. And this may not be what you want to do.

I'm sure the same thing is true for Colorado and the rest of the Rocky Mountain states. There may be other public interests that have to be addressed concerning water than simply allowing only money to move it. In its rawest form, Owens Valley was water marketing! They (Los Angeles) went up and bought all the land and water there, and today we may not want decisions to be made in that fashion. It may be that the city of Los Angeles had a higher and better use for that Owens Valley water. But I'm not sure we want decisions today made that way throughout the West. We would end up with a lot of little oases and a lot of brown areas in between.

It's one thing to have water contracts governed by statute that provide certain rights in drought conditions to recall a portion of the water. It's another thing to let those situations be governed by contracts that may not take droughts into account. So there are a lot of questions about what laws to apply to water marketing. But it does address a number of issues linked to water conservation and management that we are looking at concerning the highest and best use of this resource.

There's going to be a clash, and I can't predict the outcome. We have to start pulling it apart. I'm for water marketing, but I'm not for Noah Cross (a character in the movie *Chinatown*) being the water master to decide who's going to get it and who isn't.

Q. *What are the implications of the Westlands Water District lawsuit?* [*Westlands in California is the country's biggest water district. Farmers there are suing the Interior Department over how much it should pay for its irrigation water and*

whether it should pay anything more to resolve its drainage problems.]

A. One of our concerns is that all of the costs of these changes are not self-contained within the beneficiaries of the contract. Some of these costs overlap onto other people. The issue here is whether they are politically powerful enough to get what they want. Should they succeed, which I very much oppose, what you will see is that a lot of other irrigation districts will pay for Westlands' greed politically. Once again, Congress is going to be confronted with a district that is keeping a very substantial amount of special privilege for a very few, very wealthy people, and that's just going to taint all of Western irrigation.

— *Lawrence Mosher*

The subject was: how to get the House conferees to bend enough toward the Senate version of the omnibus water bill to avoid a presidential veto? Both the environmentalists and Dawson opposed the House bill because its cost-sharing provisions were too weak, and it was loaded down with 125 more projects than the Senate bill. The environmental groups endorsed the Senate bill because of the relatively limited number of new projects and because it would cast requirements for significant cost-sharing in legislation.

The group was told by the Corps' chief of engineers, Lt. Gen. E.R. Heiberg III, "The system now won't let you build water projects the nation needs," and no one disagreed.

A week later, the National Wildlife Federation hosted a press conference that featured a number of its former enemies, such as four retired Corps executives and representatives of the Associated General Contractors of America and the American Association of Port Authorities. Lynn Greenwalt, the NWF's vice president for resource conservation, said:

"The National Wildlife Federation cannot support the authorization of hundreds of new water projects with an estimated cost of more than $18 billion without significant cost-sharing and user-fee requirements. Those reforms are absolutely necessary for the nation to set priorities and weed out the political boondoggles from the genuinely necessary projects that represent sound investment and wise natural resource management."

Ed Osann, who lobbies Congress for the NWF, answers the question: Why would an environmental group support any water works bill? Why not go for 20 years of no new starts? First, he gives a negative reason. The Senate and House appropriations committees have indicated that "they're tired of waiting, and have tried to appropriate dollars" even without a bill authorizing new starts.

But mainly, he says, the bill represents an opportunity to institutionalize user-fees and cost-sharing that will make the construction of water projects more or less self-correcting. Local users, he says, won't put up their own money for worthless or uneconomic projects. "It's not a panacea, but it's a big step forward."

Another Washington, D.C., group that has spent much time lobbying against water projects, the Environmental Policy Institute, disagrees. Blackwelder says, "The reforms are not strong enough. But it's a judgment call. No one is sure how much cost-sharing it will take to kill a boondoggle, or encourage nonstructural solutions." His group also fears that reforms imposed at the top won't stick. "In the field the Corps will try to undercut reform."

Have 10 years of blocked water left the nation with an infrastructure gap? Are good projects mixed in among the House's list of 300, or the Senate's smaller list? Blackwelder sees no kernel of gold: "It's the same old stuff — solutions out of the 1940s."

The only need Blackwelder sees are those created by old projects. The state of Florida, for example, is spending millions to put the meanders back into the Kissimmee River, which the Corps "channelized" 20 years ago. "A re-reclamation bill — that would be interesting. It would send a different signal," Blackwelder says.

But while the environmental groups may not be unanimous in supporting even a Corps water works bill with reform provisions, support or opposition to the bill is a "judgment call." The Corps' willingness to push for user fee and cost-sharing reforms has blunted criticism and put some environmental groups in the agency's corner. Over at Interior, however, things are different.

The Beleaguered Bureau

Throughout the first four years of the Reagan administration, while the Corps was gearing up for survival, Interior's Bureau of Reclamation was refusing to acknowledge new realities. Interior Secretary James Watt fought the Corps' Gianelli at every policy turn. The fight reflected political differences that set the Corps' national constituency apart from the Bureau's 17-state Western domain.

HOW FISCAL EROSION HAS NIBBLED AT WATER AGENCIES

	ARMY CORPS OF ENGINEERS		BUREAU OF RECLAMATION	
Year	Construction	Manpower	Construction	Manpower
1977	$1,400,000	33,050	$721,042	9,180
1978	1,500,000	33,002	574,756	8,249
1979	1,300,000	32,958	401,056	8,252
1980	1,700,000	32,539	424,319	8,308
1981	1,600,000	32,745	576,115	8,139
1982	1,400,000	32,173	548,505	8,307
1983	1,500,000	30,564	636,009	8,292
1984	927,000	28,935	695,318	8,277
1985	955,000	28,645	754,300	8,103
1986	919,000	28,395	521,700	8,245

While the Bureau's local sponsors pay some money back to the federal government in 40- and 50-year obligations or through per acre-foot user fees, the federal government still ends up subsidizing the Bureau's projects in a variety of ways. These include negligible or no-interest payments, user fees that do not reflect the cost of providing the water, and long-term repayment schedules that do not reflect inflation. Watt feared that any shift toward cost-sharing by the Corps would erode the built-in subsidies of the Bureau.

With Watt gone, the Bureau has gotten out of the way of the Corps' initiatives and is itself biting the cost-sharing bullet. The agreement reached June 30, 1986, for the Animas-LaPlata project has Colorado and New Mexico interests paying 18 percent of the $379.3 million cost. Environmentalists say the cost sharing was done with mirrors, but the need to settle Indian claims to water rights gave the project broader support than it would otherwise have had.

The Bureau is not so much affected by cost sharing as by the blunt fact that it is running out of projects to build. Much of its work is devoted to finishing mammoth projects authorized years ago, such as the Central Arizona Project, which will transfer Colorado River water beyond Phoenix to Tucson, and the Central Utah Project, which will move Colorado River water from eastern Utah into the Great Salt Lake basin.

In 1986, Congress approved what may be the last of these major Bureau systems: North Dakota's Garrison Diversion Unit of the Pick-Sloan Missouri Basin Program. After decades of controversy, the House passed a pared-down version that will cost just under $1 billion. Representative George Miller, Democrat from California, whose Interior and Insular Affairs Subcommittee on Water and Power handled the compromise, made it clear Garrison was moving forward only because of strong past political commitments and the fact that a congressionally appointed commission had forged the compromise.

Even so, more federally subsidized irrigation water to produce more surplus crops triggered a spirited debate. The original bill required that farmers who choose to raise surplus crops pay a 10 percent surcharge on their water. But Representative Philip R. Sharp, Democrat from Indiana, introduced an amendment to raise the surcharge to the full cost of the water.

"It simply defies logic that today, whatever our historic approach to this has been, it makes no sense to go forward as we have in the past without saying, 'Look folks, we are not going to subsidize something that is counter to federal policy now, and is almost certain to be counter to federal policy in the future.'"

The amendment failed. But the close vote in the House – 203-199 – presages an inevitable policy shift. The Bureau has not just run out of new dam sites. By having irrigated millions of acres in the West, it has also helped bury the nation under a mountain of food, and thus made its 'reclaim the desert' mission not only unnecessary but counter to the current public interest.

Its plugging of every major river in the West, and the irrigation of millions of formerly desert acres, has also created a new, and ironic, mission for the Bureau: cleaning up messes it has made. The Bureau has been waging war with an old adversary, salt, for decades with little apparent effect. Now it faces new enemies: the mounting pollution from fertilizers and pesticides, and in California's rich San Joaquin Valley, a special culprit called selenium.

This trace element, toxic at high concentrations, is common in Western soils, including those found in the San Joaquin Valley. In 1983, the Fish and Wildlife Service, which operates a bird refuge at Kesterson Reservoir, discovered duck birth deformities and deaths. Selenium was the culprit, carried there by the San Luis Drain from 42,000 acres in the San Joaquin's Westlands Water District. On March 30, 1985, Interior Secretary Donald P. Hodel announced that the tainted drainage would cease by June 30, 1986.

Since then, the Kesterson debacle has come to spotlight the growing confusion over the Bureau's future. With new dams nowhere on the horizon, the Bureau is left only with trying to remedy the ill effects of its past work. How well is it equipped to handle re-reclamation?

Congressman Miller, whose Interior panel on water and power oversees the Bureau, views the array of problems symbolized by Kesterson as the Bureau's potential Waterloo:

"It used to be that you just put the water on the land, the land bloomed, and everyone was happy," Miller said recently. "Now we know that this also starts an event that is then played out over a long period of time, and this is now turning out to be somewhat catastrophic at Kesterson.

"The Interior Department wants to stumble along with Kesterson and the drainage problem for another decade. But our committee is rapidly losing confidence in the Bureau, and is starting to look for alternatives. Interior's agencies don't have the sense of urgency that toxics dictate you now must have. Science is showing that toxics are running faster than the bureaucracies.

"Interior will come up here and tell you how to build a dam that some congressman promised his state in 1945. But they can't seem to say how to clean up the drainage mess . . . This is their challenge, and they are running out of time."

Another drainage mess, one which began ticking with the first damming of the Colorado, is the growing salting of that now almost totally throttled river. After U.S. farmers on Reclamation projects nearly ruined Mexico's best agricultural area by sending that nation Colorado River water with 2500 parts per million of salt, Congress enacted the Colorado River Basin Salinity Control Act in 1974. Its goals were to build a desalting plant at Yuma, Arizona, and to engineer costly solutions at various, mostly upper basin, salt sources.

As Marc Reisner points out in *Cadillac Desert,* no consideration was given to the cost-effectiveness of reducing irrigation use of the Colorado, which produces 37 percent of the river's salinity.

"One could easily achieve the same results (as the desalting plant) by buying out the few thousand acres of alkaline and poorly drained land that contribute most to the problem, but there, once again, one runs up against the holiness of the blooming desert," Reisner writes.

Only in 1984 did Congress amend the 1974 law to bring in the water management ideas of the Soil Conservation Service. The SCS now notes that over half of the one million acres of irrigated land contributing the salt are correctable without expensive pipelines to run the salty water to the ocean (one plan had a pipe carrying both salt water and coal), or enormous man-made evaporation ponds (mini Great Salt Lakes) in the desert. Instead of these structural solutions, SCS tries to correct over-watering, high-surface runoff and other matters under control of the farmer. It is Backwelder's non-structural 're-reclamation,' but it is not coming from the Bureau.

While nonstructural improvements are going forward, so is the Yuma plant. When complete, it will use reverse osmosis and lots of electricity to deliver 67,000 acre-feet of water at a fairly pure 295 parts per million of salt. It will cost $210 million to build, and $333 per acre-foot of water produced. By comparison, upriver irrigators pay the Bureau $3.50 an acre-foot for water—water they often return to the river loaded with salt.

The plant should open in 1989, allowing the United States to fulfill its treaty obligations to Mexico to deliver 1,360,000 acre-feet a year of Colorado River water, with an average saltiness of no more than 115 parts per million of salt more than the water arriving at Imperial Dam for diversion to California's cities and farms.

The Future Versus the Past

You don't have to be a cost-benefit accountant to guess which federal agency is more attuned to the times. While the Corps is lining up agreements that call for 50 percent local financing of deep-draft ports, the Bureau is trying to finish up its construction agenda by spreading the financial burden around the nation.

A favorite place to stick these costs is on those who use electric power generated by Western dams. The so-called large 'cash register' dams were meant to subsidize irrigation projects farmers couldn't afford.

But NWF's Osann says the use of power revenues from Glen Canyon, Flaming Gorge, Curecanti, et al., was sleight of hand accounting. "Electric power rates aren't raised to pay for irrigation dams." According to Osann, the electric power revenues won't be diverted to pay for irrigation projects until the dam itself is paid for. Given the typical 50-year repayment schedule, that will be well into the next century. And then the irrigation projects are repaid at zero interest.

Even worse, says Osann, the hydro projects themselves are grossly subsidized, so the use of these 'cash registers' to justify building irrigation projects represents a subsidy within a subsidy.

Lately, that subsidy within a subsidy has been toned down a bit. To satisfy the fiscal squeeze, water users are letting the electric power revenue surcharges for the latest projects start flowing to the Treasury immediately. The Animas-LaPlata cost-sharing agreement signed June 30, 1986, requires Colorado River Storage Project users to pay for irrigation costs immediately, instead of 50 years from now. That will increase CRSP rates about one-tenth of a cent, or one mill. Since CRSP power is dirt cheap—a penny a kilowatt-hour—that means a 10 percent increase in rates.

The $1 billion Garrison project employed the same power revenue speedup. Pick-Sloan power customers will begin paying a share of the project costs immediately, rather than after 50 years.

And Central Arizona Project completion requires Arizona power users to pay an additional 4.5 mills on part of Hoover Dam's power.

The Bureau has tapped another source. The financing agreement for Plan 6 of the Central Arizona Project — a tradeoff for abandoning the controversial Orme Dam Project — will use federal money authorized by the Reclamation Safety of Dams Act. That law's funds are earmarked only for existing dams. Interior's Solicitor, however, contends that applying the money to build the new Cliff Dam in Plan 6 is legal because Cliff Dam replaces the authorized Orme Dam. If there is any logic there, the National Wildlife Federation fails to see it, and is attempting to block construction.

There you have the Bureau of Reclamation blueprint for survival: drill its money-siphon deeper into the public power revenue base. While the Corps has developed a practical strategy for surviving into the next century, the Bureau of Reclamation has been designing an artifice of buckpassing to hydropower consumers in order to finish its past agenda.

3

Selling Water, or Selling Out?

Bob Gottlieb

Peter Wiley

F or more than six years, environmentalists have grappled with the problem of developing strategies in the era of Ronald Reagan and the conservative retrenchment. In the area of water policy, environmentalists feared that the tentative reforms of the Carter administration would be swept aside in an avalanche of new water projects and hostility to environmental values.

To meet this challenge, certain key individuals and groups argued that an affirmative strategy was required to marry Reaganism to the goals of the environmental movement. They turned to the already existing idea of "water markets" as an idea they hoped would appeal to conservatives and also protect the environment.

The strategy worked, and today the water market concept is the hottest thing going in the arid West. It is the talk of development interests and environmentalists, conservative and liberal politicians, Bureau of Reclamation officials and Office of Management and Budget red pencilers alike. Bills have been introduced and back rooms are rife with talk of entitlement transfers, sale/leaseback arrangements and other trade-offs that evoke the now sacrosanct free market.

To conservatives, water markets are economic transactions, pure and simple. But to most environmentalists, markets imply something

else: greater efficiency in water use, which means fewer new dams. They also see additional environmental safeguards built into the water deals. Overall, it is clear that markets create "winners." But are there no "losers"? Does everybody win, as claims Tom Graff, a leading water-market advocate attorney for the Environmental Defense Fund?

A water-market transaction can take place in a number of ways, ranging from the sale of a ranch along with its water rights, to more complex leasing or to the separation of land from its water. In states such as Colorado or Utah, there have always been water markets of a sort. During the synfuels boom of the late 1970s, agricultural interests sold water, usually with the land still attached, to oil companies and speculators who helped drive the price at least as high as $1,750 an acre-foot.

But those transactions are the exceptions. In almost all cases, water rights and entitlements have been based not on market principles, but on politically crafted water allocation systems, much of it in the form of federal programs. The ongoing construction of the Central Arizona Project and the Central Utah Project are driven by congressional appropriations of billions of dollars. They are political projects, with political distribution of the resulting water.

This political system, some charge, is inefficient and inequitable, favoring large users such as agriculture, which uses more than 85 percent of the water in most Western states. Federal Reclamation projects, with built-in subsidies originally intended to further the family farm in the West, brought more land under cultivation. But in many cases, especially in California, they also led to the concentration of land ownership in the hands of large operators.

Within this system of public subsidies, there have been clear winners and losers. Large agricultural interests and urban developers operating in some outlying areas have been big winners. Losers have included federal taxpayers, inner city urban interests, small farmers squeezed by concentration and overproduction, and the environment. Free-flowing rivers and streams have especially suffered, as they became dammed, ditched and diverted.

By the 1960s, this publicly subsidized and regulated system reached its height. Proposals could still be heard for giant multi-billion-dollar water transfer projects stretching from Alaska to the Great Plains to the Mexican border. At the same time, criticism began to surface, particularly among certain academics. A seminal study in 1965, *Northern California's Water Supply*, put forth for the first time in a detailed way the notion that water markets might correct the system's inefficiencies. A water market, the argument went, would make it more profitable for those farming marginal lands with imported water to sell their cheap subsidized water to the highest bidder, such as a nearby urban area.

During the 1970s, the water market idea got little attention. Instead of seeking efficiency through free markets, water leaders continued to press for politically subsidized water projects. Then came the election of Ronald Reagan and the referendum defeat of California's Peripheral Canal project—two events that dramatically influenced both the water industry and environmentalists.

Soon after his election, it became clear that hope for new projects was misplaced, despite pro-development and anti-environmental rhetoric from Secretary of Interior James Watt and Reclamation Commissioner Robert Broadbent. Instead, talk of cost-sharing with the states and a squeeze on existing authorized projects dominated the first Reagan term, almost as if a more combative Carter had been re-elected.

To their surprise, conservation groups, which were rapidly gaining members, found themselves on the offensive. In this context, the water market idea resurfaced. Under the leadership of Tom Graff and Zach Willey of the Environmental Defense Fund, the idea was seen as a way to appeal to conservatives while strengthening environmental protection.

A clear indication that the desire for environmental protection was still strong in the land came in California's referendum mentioned above. For more than 15 years after construction had first begun on the California Aqueduct, Central Valley and Southern California water development interests had been coveting a Peripheral Canal to increase the project's yield. Stymied through two terms of Governor Reagan, the water interests, in conjunction with his successor Jerry Brown, came up with a package that traded off water development for limited environmental protection.

Some environmental leaders argued that the package was the best deal possible. But the vast majority of enviromentalists disagreed. With the help of a split in the water industry and an inspired campaign that undercut the consensus for development in the southern part of the state, they produced 90 percent majorities against the canal in the north. The package was defeated by more than 3 to 2.

The vote only involved Californians. But California is the major water developer in the West. California inspired the Colorado River Compact and the Hoover Dam. California interests drained Owens Valley and built the California and Colorado River aqueducts. The defeat of the Peripheral Canal by Californians could only mean that water politics would never again be the same.

Three extraordinary events reinforced the change. The first involved the Imperial Irrigation District (IID). During the Peripheral Canal campaign, the California Department of Water Resources reported that IID was wasting an enormous amount of Colorado River water — 438,000 acre-feet a year — due to such things as unlined canals. A mix of lawsuits, media attention, and threatened action by the state placed the District in a politically difficult situation.

The Imperial District's problems had become an issue for urban Southern California as well. Critics of the Peripheral Canal had argued that the Metropolitan Water District of Southern California (MWD is the Big Daddy of water wholesalers in the area) didn't need the canal; it could "find" alternative sources of supply by measures as simple as paying for conservation.

In 1981 and 1982, when the idea first surfaced, both districts strongly denied such a deal was possible. Two years later, as political and legal pressure on IID's waste mounted, the two bodies began to negotiate.

A third party interested in the trade was a member of MWD — the San Diego County Water Authority. San Diego, which at times is 90 percent dependent on water it imports from the MWD, had been a leader in the fight for the Peripheral Canal. The authority spent $625,000 on advertising to tell people that, without the canal, San Diego would run out of water in less than 20 years. The defeat of the canal set San Diego's water managers to wondering if it needed to look for its own water.

The situation was ripe for a fast-talking Louisiana speculator/entrepreneur named Doyle G. Berry. During the synfuels boom, Berry and associates, known as the Galloway Group, had bought Colorado

River basin water rights in Colorado. They anticipated selling them to synfuel companies, but they didn't anticipate the collapse of oil shale.

When that happened, the group began seeking other buyers. It approached San Diego with a proposal: build a hydroelectric dam on Colorado's free-flowing Yampa River and thereby establish a beneficial use. Then pay off the Upper Basin states (Colorado, Utah, Wyoming, and New Mexico) in the Colorado River system, as well as Arizona in the Lower Basin, for use of their entitlements.

The idea, the Galloway Group hoped, would appeal to the Upper Basin states. They are not yet using their full allocated share of the Colorado River, and with the sharp decline in agriculture, mining, and energy in the Upper Basin states, the day seems far off when those states would impound and use that water. Instead, the Upper Basin states' share of the water continues to flow downstream. At present, California gets to use much of that surplus. When the Central Arizona Project is in full operation, some of the unused Upper Basin water will flow there. In any case, the Upper Basin gets no benefit from that water except to watch it flow past.

The idea of 300,000 to 500,000 acre-feet of water caused San Diego to jump at the offer and pay a $10,000 option on the deal. Then all hell broke loose. The Southern California MWD staff was livid. They said the deal violated the Colorado River Compact and other agreements collectively known as the Law of the River. They argued that a MWD member was trying to buy surplus Colorado River water that would otherwise flow to the district as a whole.

At first, nearly everyone in the water industry supported MWD. Even environmentalists, who were promoting the market idea, were aghast at damming the Yampa. But within a year, the consensus shifted. Talk centered less on the specific Galloway proposal than on San Diego's growing commitment to buy water from those who either didn't need it or found it profitable to sell. The Galloway idea wasn't going anywhere but the water market idea survived.

San Diego especially toyed with purchasing water from agriculture. The Authority made known its interest in the IID situation, hinting that it might pay a lot more than the MWD, much to the latter's dismay. San Diego also began to talk to parties in the Central Valley, including corporate farmers such as Tenneco. Those landowners had, by 1984 and 1985, become much more receptive to the market idea.

The handful of corporations that control two-thirds of the state water in the Kern area had profited enormously over the previous 15 years, due to their cheap California Aqueduct water. By comparison, urban residents who got their water from the MWD were paying higher rates because the MWD's water from the project was much more expensive than agriculture's water. The system was designed to have urban users subsidize agriculture. In this case, though, the subsidy wasn't going to the family farm; it was going to enormous corporate farms.

But cheap water and corporate treasuries weren't enough. By 1985, the farm crisis had reached Kern County. Talk of default or return of the water entitlements, cheap as they were, surfaced. Some of the biggest corporate farmers — Tenneco, Tejon Ranch, and the George W. Nickel interests — indicated a desire to get out of farming, and approaches were made to San Diego and MWD. The Kern situation had transformed several major agricultural players from critics to supporters of water markets, especially in light of its bail-out possibilities.

A few general principles underlie the situation where marketing has been considered. In each of the episodes described, outside political or economic pressures created the impetus for discussion. Moreover, at least in these cases, water marketing is not free of environmental or equity problems: one plan would build an unnecessary

Tom Graff, Environmental Defense Fund

dam; another would bail out and thereby further subsidize corporate landowners passing as farmers.

For environmentalists such as EDF's Graff, there will always be tension between those who advocate markets as an economic transaction and those, like EDF, who say any deals have to contain provisions to protect the environment. Graff also argues that although subsidies may exist in any buy-out, the market idea is the quickest way to change the status quo by transferring water from farms to cities.

There are other ways to change the status quo—some, such as the Natural Resources Defense Council, urge that the interest rates on the projects be raised, thereby removing some of the water subsidy to farms and likely retiring production on marginal lands. That in turn would reduce overall water use. But Graff says such reform is very slow, at best, given agriculture's continuing political power.

The question of winners and losers in water market deals is also the question of future water development. If, by creating water markets, marginal lands are retired because farmers sell water, then there is more water in the system and less pressure to build new dams and ditches. This is no small feat.

But it is possible that we are in the midst of an historic economic shift that will force corporate landowners out of farming without water-market deals. In that case, the water market would be just another subsidy. There is also no reason to believe environmental protection will be built into water market deals unless political pressure is applied. Why not, then, apply that pressure to raise interest costs to agriculture, accomplish the same goal, and put the subsidy/bail-out option to rest?

Those choices relate to the way environmentalists assess the strength of their position. It suggests different ways of meeting the quandary of Reaganism: by action and political pressure, or by adopting a free market strategy. It comes down to the analysis of whether the free market for water is just one more boondoggle, or an avenue for change in a transitional political era.

4

When Water Kingdoms Clash

Ed Marston

O ver the next decade, the millions who live in the southern California megalopolis centered on Los Angeles will lose 650,000 acre-feet of water now available to them out of the Colorado River. That water will be diverted away from the 46-year-old Colorado River Aqueduct and into the spanking-new $3.6 billion Central Arizona Project as ordained by interstate agreements and court decisions.

The loser of this water is the Metropolitan Water District, or Met, a vast public entity that supplies water to 5200 square miles of homes, lawns, swimming pools, car washes, cemeteries, offices and industry in six sprawling yet densely settled southern California counties.

Whether the Met can cope with the loss of enough water to supply 1.5 million people will determine if its service territory can expand at a projected 180,000 people per year. How it copes with the loss will determine the fate of the hottest, perhaps the only, new idea to hit Western water in decades — water marketing.

In pure form, water marketing is the treating of water as a commodity to be bought and sold on the basis of supply and demand. In most areas of life, a marketplace for commodities is the rule. In Western water, it is revolutionary.

For example, the Met's first reaction to the looming loss of water to Arizona was not to seek water to buy. It sought instead to bring in 'new' water from northern California by building the Peripheral Canal. The construction of long canals or big dams to obtain more water is the traditional response of institutions that control water in the West. But California voters barred construction of the Peripheral Canal in a 1982 referendum, and set the stage for a test of water marketing.

Literally next door to the Met's urban 5200 square-mile territory are one million acres (1700 square miles) of desert ministered to by the Imperial Irrigation District. Half of the land, 500,000 acres, grows crops year-around, thanks to Colorado River water.

Without the Colorado River, the Imperial Valley would be desert. It lies several hundred feet below sea level, has 100 days when the temperature hits at least 100 degrees, has no usable groundwater, and gets three inches of rainfall a year. But with its 2.5 million acre-feet of Colorado River water — one-sixth of the river's yearly flow — the Imperial Valley is one of the world's most productive farm areas.

A desert farmer's religion is that he can never have enough water. But that belief is being challenged in the Imperial Valley. In the early part of this century, jerry-built efforts to divert the Colorado let it escape its natural channel to the Gulf of California, and pour unchecked into the Imperial Valley. By the time it was recaptured, its flow had transformed a dry sink at the low point in the valley into the Salton Sea. Today that sea functions as a catchment for irrigation water that doesn't evaporate or get taken up by plants. As a result, the Salton Sea has grown steadily over the decades.

In 1980, a farmer adjacent to the sea tired of building dikes to protect his farmland against the rising water. The five-man Imperial Irrigation District board wasn't interested in his problem, so he turned to the state bureaucracy for help. In 1984, he got it. The State Water Resources Control Board ruled that Imperial and its farmers were wasting water, and that the wasted water was causing the Salton Sea to rise. A state study showed that by spending several hundred million dollars to line ditches and take other steps, the waste could be stopped.

In California, wasting water is a literal crime. Although Imperial is fighting the decision, the ruling has put pressures on it to stop letting its water seep through its dirt ditches, and to stop its farmers from sloshing too much water onto their fields. Studies show Imperial could save about 440,000 acre-feet (3 percent of the Colorado's flow and enough water to supply 1.2 million people) while still keeping its 500,000 acres green.

Imperial could use the wasted water to irrigate 100,000 more acres of desert. But that is the last thing its farmers want. Alfalfa, the stuff of hay and the valley's top crop, has fallen drastically in price; the market for another major crop, cotton, is in sad shape.

Moreover, the saving of water beyond the 100,000 acre-feet or so already conserved would require money Imperial doesn't have. That combination of circumstances appeared to set the stage for a water sale, lease, condominiumization or dry-year insurance agreement, between Imperial and the Met.

Such a deal had been studied and promoted for years by the Environmental Defense Fund. But the person who got things into motion was a picaresque businessman named Tom Havens. Havens is attractive and energetic, and his all-American entrepreneurism gained him the ear of Imperial's five-man board. Havens, in an August 1986 interview, said he saw immediately that he faced a major cultural problem — the tendency of Imperial's farmers to distrust L.A.'s city slickers.

They had good reason for fear. According to Havens, Imperial, secure in its very senior water rights and in its fertile desert land,

Tom Havens

hadn't made itself an integral part of the California water network. It had stayed to itself. It wasn't politically or economically savvy, and so it wasn't ready to start cutting deals.

"The Imperial Valley has 100,000 people living in the desert. There is a pitchfork mentality there," said Havens.

By comparison, "The Met is like a laser beam. It is well organized. It has a large staff. It can task-force 200 people on a project in a matter of days. It can intimidate, control and dominate every water district and water attorney in California."

Moreover, the Met informally heads a network of California water boards. "They are good at exerting power, but they don't have imagination. The typical age of California water board members is 65, and until now nothing had ever changed. A 65-year-old appreciates the past. The future is dark, depressing, uncertain."

Havens said he convinced Imperial's board that it needed "an army to supplement your pitchforks." In preparation for the wheeling and dealing, Imperial brought in as general manager a 30-year veteran of the Army Corps of Engineers named Charles Shreves.

The board, at Havens' suggestion, found an army in the person of Parsons Water Resources. Parsons, an immense engineering and construction firm, has hit hard times due to the disappearance of the mega-projects it had specialized in building. The forces that had defeated the Peripheral Canal and created the time for water marketing had also sent Parsons in search of work in privatization, efficiency, and conservation.

Parsons' Imperial task force, headed by another Army Corps veteran, Joe Bratton, was to do the legal and engineering work needed if Imperial was to negotiate on an equal basis with the Met. And, in Havens' mind at least, Parsons was to play big brother to Imperial, lending the district its political and negotiating muscle. For his matchmaking, Havens said he was promised a share in future income from a water sale.

The Imperial-Parsons relationship started out bravely, with Parsons talking of the new world of efficiency and conservation. And in 1985, a non-binding memorandum of understanding between Imperial and the Met came close to adoption. The Met was to get the use of 100,000 acre-feet a year of Imperial's water. And it was to pay Imperial $10 million a year to line ditches and generally conserve water now flowing into the Salton Sea. The $10 million works out to $100 a year per acre-foot. But both sides said the water wasn't being bought and sold. The Met was giving Imperial money to conserve water, and in return getting the use of the saved water.

The proposed deal caused political stress that the Imperial board couldn't withstand; in June, 1986, two critics were elected to the five-

person board. A key part of the unrest was due to Parsons, which became a villain locally. Although the firm came in saying it would share in the risks of the game, it charged Imperial several million dollars to do an efficiency study critics said merely rehashed old reports.

Under pressure, Imperial backed away from Parsons and the $100 an acre-foot deal. After formal public hearings and numerous coffee-shop conversations, the board decided its water was worth $250 an acre-foot, plus built-in escalators for inflation. Then, in August, Imperial made its inability to cope with water marketing official by breaking off all negotiations.

Havens blames the collapse on Parsons, which, he said, couldn't adapt to Imperial's needs. "In the past, Parsons' clients told it what to do." In this case, Parsons had to show the way. "But it's not their culture to be innovative or entrepreneurial."

Instead of leading the Imperial Valley out of the desert, Havens said, "The psychology that has been allowed to develop by Imperial and Parsons has been fear—fear of receiving $90 million a year for their water . . . . Imperial's mentality is to not give up a drop of water under any circumstances. I think that's death. And Parsons chose to do Imperial's bidding."

Havens said negotiations were also handicapped because both Imperial and the Parsons task force were led by Army Corps of Engineers veterans. "They're used to having lots of staff, lots of preparation for a decision. They're both far from what the marketplace needs."

For the moment, the Met appears content to watch Imperial squirm while the law against waste water tightens around it. The Met can afford to wait. Wet years have kept the river full. Moreover, the urban water supply district sees lots of eager sellers out there. For example, corporate farmers in the Kern Valley, who use water imported from northern California, would love to unload it on the cities.

Although the impasse seems to say that water marketing is not yet here, it is also true that no one is pushing the Peripheral Canal. Water transfers in some form appear to be the solution of choice.

But the Imperial-Met brawl also shows that water is not just another economic commodity. Politics are still there, only now it is local and regional politics rather than federal politics.

5

Shrink to Fit

Douglas Towne

I n Colorado, California is still used as a boogeyman to scare up support for expensive water projects. The would-be dam-builders say: If we don't build this, California will take our water."

But in California, the boogeyman is the spectre of too much water, and "stealing" Colorado's water has a relatively low priority these days. The failure of the Peripheral Canal referendum in 1982, which blocked further export of northern California water to the south, was to have set off a rush to grab more Colorado River water. The huge Metropolitan Water District, which supplies water to southern California's sprawling urban areas, was to lead the rush, Colorado water experts warned.

Things haven't worked out that way. Instead, the MWD has been inundated by would-be sellers of agricultural water from the nearby irrigated inland valleys. In fact, the California boogeyman is that of a WPPSS-like financial debacle. (WPPSS, the acronym for the Washington Public Power Supply System, is pronounced Whoops.) But instead of nuclear power plants, this WPPSS, speculates Tom Graff of the Environmental Defense Fund in Berkeley, could be the California Water Project.

The California Water Project brought northern California water south to urbanites and to corporate farmers in Kern Valley. The urban users subsidize the irrigation water, but even so Kern Valley's corporate farmers can't make a go of it.

Graff speculates that eventually state government will have to decide how to bail out the California Water Project. A buy-out by the MWD may be one route to a bail-out. But MWD's urban customers are already paying more than their share for the water brought from the north, and they may balk.

Kern Valley's agricultural troubles are statistically visible. Ten to 15 percent of the land that was irrigated a few years ago lies fallow today. A one million acre-foot per year groundwater overdraft has become a 3.5 million acre-foot replenishment of underlying aquifers. (Kern Valley agriculture is served by both pumped groundwater and imported surface water.)

Some of that replenishment is due to unusually wet years. But much is due to the kind of fundamental economic changes that created WPPSS, that left the West with an enormous electric power surplus, that closed copper, coal, and molybdenum mines in the region, and that killed plans for various grandiose water and natural resource developments throughout the West.

Southern California is complicated: It is made up of corporate farmers with deep pockets, subsidized water, the most fertile land in the world, 365-day growing seasons and proximity to enormous urban markets. These factors give the area's agriculture enormous inertia that tends to delay the visibility of trends.

By comparison, the irrigated farming region in the valleys of southeastern Arizona has little institutional, political or private muscle to withstand the blowing of fresh economic winds. The lack of inertia is immediately apparent on an evening visit to the Arizona hamlet of Kansas Settlement. This community in the shadow of the Dragoon Mountains once supplied services to the farmers in Sulphur Springs Valley. Now, all is dark and still. The only signs of life are a few lighted farmhouses dotting the surrounding landscapes.

The faded words "Sodbuster Bar and Grill" can be seen on one of the abandoned buildings, sign of a bygone era of expansion. A broken Lucky Lager Beer neon light dangles from the roof; tumbleweeds block the entrance to the decrepit but intact building. Like the remaining farms in the vicinity, it is near collapse but still standing.

In Cochise County, Arizona, which includes the Sulphur Springs Valley and other farming areas, only 22 percent of the irrigated farmland in 1976 was still in production in 1983. From a peak of 171,400 acres, the irrigated land dropped to 38,640 acres. And abandonment continues.

Much of the cropland being abandoned came into production in the 1960s, when cheap land prices for cotton and grain attracted farmers from Texas. The acres they brought into cultivation were generally not prime agricultural land, and the need to irrigate more and often poorer land depleted the underlying aquifers.

So, southeastern Arizona, like many irrigated lands in the West, experienced dropping aquifer levels and rising energy costs to pump up water from ever deeper levels. The average cost per acre-foot of water pumped using natural gas in the Kansas Settlement area increased from $25 in 1975 to $80 in 1985. Water must be drawn up from a depth approaching 500 feet. The pumping costs, a rise in interest rates, expensive tractors, the high cost of chemical farming, and dropping commodity prices combined to drive 78 percent of the irrigated land out of production.

The evidence of that abandoned land is visible in the form of rusting irrigation pumps and barren or weed-infested fields that a few years ago were covered by cotton, grains, and sorghum. Lacking any natural cover, these fields of sandy and loamy soils fall prey to erosion,

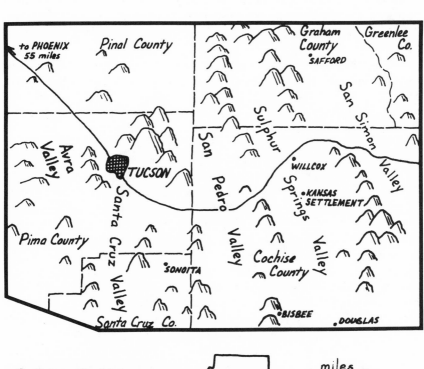

SOUTHEAST ARIZONA

ARIZONA

miles
0   10   20

adapted by Mary Moran
from a map by Douglas Towne

dust, and weeds. "What we're doing is creating very dramatic desert areas," says Martin Karpiscak, a researcher in the University of Arizona's Office of Arid Land Studies.

It is difficult to get anything but tumbleweed to grow on this dry, often saline soil. Karpiscak says the best revegetation occurs on farms whose irrigation systems still work. But most irrigation systems are inoperable because of disuse and lack of parts. And there is the problem of who will pay to pump groundwater onto abandoned fields. Farmers usually aren't concerned or can't afford the costs, and government assistance is minimal.

The area has not always been in crops. Ranching became the dominant economic activity when settlers arrived in the 1870s, and found the lush grassland on the valley floors. Livestock grazing flourished, and the town of Willcox soon became one of the leading cattle shipping centers of the nation.

Interest in farming started when unusually heavy rains prompted a group of homesteaders to plant crops in 1905. When rainfall returned to normal, farmers turned to groundwater, and over the decades irrigated farmland took over more and more grazing land as the efficiency of pump motors increased, making irrigation more economic.

In theory, the area could return to ranching, or be used for wildlife habitat. But reseeding for livestock grazing rarely makes economic sense, and the incentive for conservation practices and weed control is weak. Livestock operators do lease abandoned farmland and graze cattle on it to keep the weeds down. But the cattle increase erosion and dust and interfere with the natural cycle of vegetative succession; some think they may do more harm than good over the long run.

Farmers around Tucson face many of the same problems found in Sulphur Springs Valley. But they have a resource the Sulphur Springs farmers lack: There is urban demand for their water and land. Because Tucson and the farmers in the Avra and Santa Cruz valleys pump from the same aquifer, the city has purchased and retired 13,000 acres of farmland to acquire the accompanying rights. Although this means the outlook for farming is bleak, at least farmers have a market for the land and water, something that isn't true in the sparsely populated basin and range valleys of southeastern Arizona.

Not all farmers have given up on farming around Kansas Settlement, although those who are still hanging in there don't always claim they are rational. Dan Dunagan, who owns one of the surviving farms around Kansas Settlement, says, "I'm a farming addict. Once it gets in you, it doesn't go away."

But there are also rational grounds for optimism, and it doesn't stem from some scheme to extend Central Arizona Project water south and east from Tucson. It comes instead from changes in philosophy and practice.

Instead of attempting to get maximum production from the greatest number of acres, some now farm only their best soils in an attempt to get the most yield per acre at the lowest expense. There is also a shift to higher value crops that need less water.

High-water-use crops such as cotton, sorghum and grains are being replaced by fruit and nut crops with a high economic return. Pecans, apples, peaches, pistachios, and grapes are the main new crops.

Dunagan grew up growing cotton, and it remains his favorite crop. But cotton costs him $200 an acre for water alone. He investigated less water-intensive crops and decided to plant wine grapes. Young plants can be drip-irrigated (a tiny tube sends water to each individual plant; traditional irrigation methods flood the entire field) for about $15 an acre; even mature plants will cost no more than $50 an acre.

Wine grapes are becoming an important crop in the Southwest; many vineyards have sprung up in Arizona, New Mexico, Texas and Colorado. The industry has grown to the point that the four vineyards near the town of Sonoita were granted official viticultural area status. That gives them the right to use the name "Sonoita" on their wine labels and, hopefully, build consumer loyalty.

These crops are expanding in the southeastern Arizona valleys because they have several advantages. Some of their advantages are economic: They can use the more efficient drip irrigation systems and they are being brought into production at a time when land prices are depressed. But they also have natural advantages. They are better adapted to the region's higher elevation, which means more rain and lower temperatures than found in other areas of Arizona.

But there are constraints: a large initial investment, a lag between that investment and the first yields from the trees or grapevines, and a lack of available local credit. Together, these conditions favor outside investors over the local farmer who has been raising cotton or grain.

Nevertheless, those who have stayed here are optimistic that agriculture in the region's broad north to south trending valleys — between mountains that explorer John Wesley Powell once described as "100 caterpillars crawling north from Mexico" — will survive. They say that improved use of water, the reduced amount of land in production, and the new crops are finally in tune with the region's water resources, soil and climate.

Earl Moser, a farmer near Willcox, has noticed in recent years that the water level in his wells has risen. He believes the rise stems from the large amount of abandoned cropland — land he thinks was marginal and should never have been put to the plow. "What we've got left is the best land with the best water."

Part Two

The Columbia River: An Age of Reform

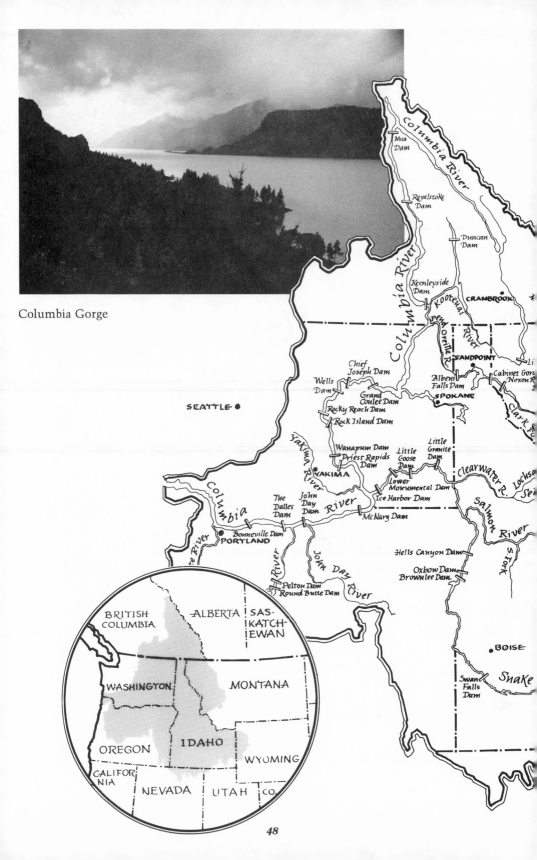

Columbia Gorge

Mica Dam

Revelstoke Dam

Duncan Dam

Keenleyside Dam

CRANBROOK

Columbia River

Kootenai River

Pend Oreille R.

SANDPOINT

Li

Chief Joseph Dam

Wells Dam

Albeni Falls Dam

Cabinet Gor Noxon R.

SEATTLE

Grand Coulee Dam

Rocky Reach Dam

Rock Island Dam

SPOKANE

Clark Fo

Yakima River

YAKIMA

Wanapum Dam

Priest Rapids Dam

Little Goose Dam

Little Granite Dam

Clearwater R. Lochsa

Lower Monumental Dam

Ice Harbor Dam

Salmon River

Se

Columbia

The Dalles Dam

John Day Dam

River

McNary Dam

S. Fork

River

Bonneville Dam

PORTLAND

John Day River

Hells Canyon Dam

Oxbow Dam
Brownlee Dam

Pelton Dam
Round Butte Dam

BRITISH COLUMBIA

ALBERTA

SAS-
KATCH-
EWAN

BOISE

Snake

Swan
Falls
Dam

WASHINGTON

MONTANA

OREGON

IDAHO

WYOMING

CALIFOR-
NIA

NEVADA

UTAH

CO.

Clark Fork Valley, Montana

Hells Canyon Dam on the Snake River, Idaho-Oregon border

COLUMBIA RIVER BASIN

River Length (miles)	Basin Size (square miles)	Average Annual Runoff (acre-feet)	Average Flow at River Mouth (acre-feet)
1,214	258,500	182.5 million	185 million

Irrigated Land (acres)	Reservoir Storage — Active Capacity (acre-feet)	Hydropower Capacity (megawatts)
7.0 million	41 million	22,000

6

The Stuff of Moral Tales

Ed Marston

Almost since the 1805 voyage of discovery by Lewis and Clark, rivers and streams in the Northwest's Columbia River basin have been mined. Salmon have been overfished, timber over-cut, and water fouled. The final insult to the Columbia River was its transformation into a series of lakes by a chain of federally built dams.

This post-World War II Era of Federalism has created enormous amounts of cheap hydroelectric power, large expanses of irrigated desert lands, locks and canals that have made Lewiston, Idaho, an ocean port, and intense logging.

The federally financed development of the Columbia River basin fed on itself and created an apparent need for ever more electricity. That led to the multibillion dollar attempt to build five large nuclear power plants. The resulting debacle, combined with other economic and social changes, created what could be called an Era of Reform.

The focus of reform is the salmon, an extraordinary fish whose spawning requires clean, cold, pure mountain streams in the upper reaches of the basin, a flow of unpolluted and sufficient water to carry the young salmon downstream to the ocean and conditions to let the adult salmon survive several years in the ocean. It then needs a fighting chance at making it back upstream to spawn in its home gravel bed.

For 100 years the salmon has been sacrificed to overfishing, and its habitat has been traded away for logging, irrigation, dams, canal and lock building, and pollution. The salmon's habitat must stretch, unbroken, for thousands of miles, so no one county, state, or nation could protect the fish, or had incentive to do so. By all logic, the salmon should be doomed. Instead, thanks to the Northwest's fishing tribes and an independent judiciary, the fish is on its way back. The story of that recovery is the stuff of which moral tales are made.

Reform, however, is hanging on by fingernails. The tribes fear that they, and the fish they have fought for, will be overwhelmed by greed, development, and racism.

Reformers worry that the welter of laws, treaties, and jurisdictions supposedly dedicated to saving the salmon will instead mangle the recovery effort. In the upper basin, the timber industry and the road-minded Forest Service threaten the spawning beds with silt. A huge output of hatchery fish could create a monocultural zoo — a vast stocked preserve for fishermen — instead of bringing back a tough, adapted natural population of salmon.

The human efforts to bring back the salmon have been Herculean. But those efforts might have been for naught without the reversal of an historical tide. That tide ran strongly for development from the latter part of the 1800s until the 1970s; its reversal has become visible only in the last few years.

The shift is most clear in the case of electric energy. The effort begun in the 1970s to build five Washington Public Power Supply System (WPPSS) nuclear power plants in the Northwest is part of history. Four plants are cancelled or mothballed, and the story of WPPSS is one of gross miscalculation of future electric power needs, corrupt contractors, incompetent workers, defaulted bonds, and a let-the-good-times-roll attitude that led to disaster.

But even the sinking of billions into non-producing power plants couldn't bring a supply and demand balance to the region's electric power market. Despite the loss of 80 percent of the planned nuclear power, continuing changes in its economy and increased conservation have left the Northwest with a surplus.

It had been exporting the surplus to California. But that market is drying up thanks to new power plants (started before the West's glut became apparent) in the Southwest and to conservation. In the Northwest itself, the region's big electric consumers — the aluminum smelters — are in trouble. Logging is on the ropes. Irrigation agriculture in the arid parts of the Columbia basin is in the same trouble as elsewhere.

In the short run, the Northwest's electric power glut is hurting the effort to recover fish and wildlife. The Bonneville Power Administration, the region's federal electric energy distributor, is squeezed for funds and is cutting back on its building of fish ladders and other recovery steps.

Should the glut continue — prolonged by conservation, as well as by power plants kept in service through improved maintenance and less use — then the time may come when economics puts a different value on the river basin's resources.

It is said that those who gaze into crystal balls end up chewing on ground glass. Certainly that has been the experience of the experts who predicted an ever-increasing need for power in the Northwest. What are those experts saying today? The conventional wisdom is that the West is experiencing a particularly deep slide in the market for all commodities. When that slide ends, in a year or two, the pendulum, it is said, will reverse and the market for aluminum, for logs, for food from irrigated agriculture will come back. At that point, the camphor will be blown away from the mothballed WPPSS plants and the Columbia's hydroelectric turbines will again be spun for every possible kilowatt.

But it is also possible that the pendulum, whose reversal the experts expect momentarily, has only begun its swing away from commodities and the kind of water development practiced by the Army Corps of Engineers and Bureau of Reclamation. If that is true, economists in the 1990s may put more long-term value on a salmon fishery and free-flowing river stretches than on kilowatt-hours, irrigated fields, and barge canals.

Ten years ago there was no talk of re-reclamation, of the decommissioning of dams and the de-channelizing of rivers. Only Native Americans and some impractical idealists believed the salmon fishery could be brought back, and they saw that happening only by learning to live with dams, barge canals, and irrigated agriculture. Today, guided not so much by environmental commitment as by new economic realities, re-reclamation is a possible future.

7

A Great Loneliness
of the Spirit

Charles F. Wilkinson

Daniel Keith Conner

And what is there to life if a man cannot hear a lovely cry of a whippoorwill or the arguments of the frogs around a pond at night? For all things share the same breath — the beasts, the trees, the man. The white man must treat the beasts of this land as his brothers. What is man without the beasts? If all beasts were gone, man would die from a great loneliness of spirit, for whatever happens to the beast also happens to the man. All things are connected. Whatever befalls the earth befalls the sons of the earth.

— Chief Seattle, letter to
President Franklin Pierce, 1855

On August 13, 1805, after several weeks of near starvation while seeking a route over the Continental Divide, Captain Meriwether Lewis enjoyed an appetizing meal. Guests of a small band of Shoshoni Indians on the Lemhi River in what is now Idaho, Lewis and Clark had been seeking evidence that they had indeed crossed the Great Divide. It was Captain Lewis's supper that convinced him: a piece of fresh roasted salmon, which he ate "with a very good relish."

On their journey down the Snake and Columbia rivers, Lewis and Clark everywhere saw evidence of the salmon economy on which the

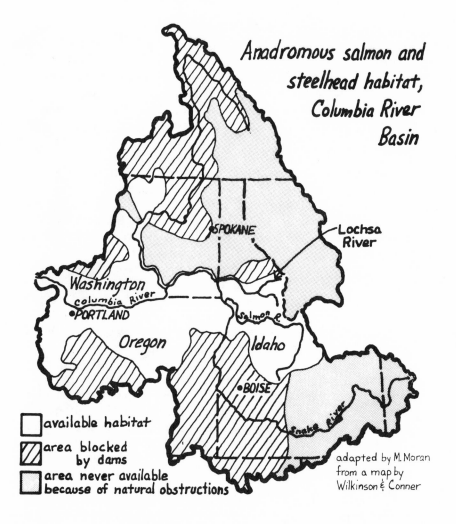

Anadromous salmon and steelhead habitat, Columbia River Basin

adapted by M. Moran from a map by Wilkinson & Conner

livelihood of Northwest Indian tribes was based. Reaching the Columbia River on October 17, Clark recorded that the water was "crouded with salmon." He added, "The number of dead Salmon on the shores & floating in the river is incredible to say. . ." Chinook salmon were then at the height of their fall run, and the astounded explorers were witnessing a natural spectacle that drew much comment in the journals and memoirs of early explorers and settlers of the Pacific Northwest.

By any standard of measure, Pacific salmon and their relative the steelhead trout are an ideal symbol of the bounty of nature: large, extravagantly numerous in their natural state, perpetually self-renewing, and easily caught. Virtually every river on the Pacific coast of North America, from Monterey Bay in California up to Alaska's Bering Peninsula, once teemed with salmon fighting their way upstream from the ocean to spawn. Late in the 19th century, old-timers would gather to swap tales of those Arcadian times when one could walk across a river on the backs of migrating fish. One crusty old liar named Hathaway Jones — a regional Munchausen of Oregon folklore who lived on a remote stretch of the Rogue River — out-classed them all by telling of the steelhead run of 1882 when the fish were so thick in the riverbed that there was no room for water.

Throughout the 19th century and well into the 20th the Columbia basin produced more salmon than any other river system in the world. No one alive today will ever see salmon runs so wondrous as those observed by William Clark or Hathaway Jones (much less the ones he lied about). Today the fabled salmon and steelhead runs are gone from more than half of their former Columbia basin habitat, and are severely depleted in the rest. Indeed, no fish anywhere has been so intensively exploited as Columbia basin salmonid species. Both nature and humans make extreme demands on them, and for that reason salmon have been called the world's most harassed fish.

If the Pacific salmon is a symbol of natural bounty, it also stands as a testament to the eagerness with which humans have sacrificed wild animals on the altar of economic development. The plight of these fish illustrates an unfortunate irony of conservation policy: In former eras society compounded the conflicts between economic develop-ment and resource conservation by providing too little regulation of common-pool resources; today, on the other hand, we overregulate them with a proliferation of uncoordinated laws in which too many government bodies have a hand.

A combination of circumstances makes Columbia basin salm-onids uniquely vulnerable to over-exploitation, to habitat degradation or to bad management.

First, a strong consumer preference makes the salmon fishery one of the world's most valuable, with a yearly catch of some 400,000 metric tons.

Second, all salmonid species are prized sport fish, and the yearly pursuit of a tackle-busting steelhead trout approaches a cult religion in the fervor and dedication of its practitioners.

Third, humans have used the fish's compelling migratory instinct to its detriment. Migrating salmonids are not easily deflected from their course; stretch a net or a trap in front of them and they will blunder right into it in a singleminded determination to make their way upstream. So eager are the fish to leap obstacles in their upriver journey that with a little skill they can practically be induced to jump into a bucket.

Fourth, migrating salmonids just before spawning tend to congregate in concentrations that lend a degree of credibility to the tales of the 19th century yarnspinners. In former times they could be scooped up almost a dozen at a time, an open invitation to excess. There are people alive who, as farmboys, simply waded into spawning streams and flipped the big fish up on the banks with pitchforks.

Finally, the extraordinary migratory habits of salmon and steelhead have worked against them in a way that places the demands of nature in conflict with human institutions. Some species of Columbia basin salmonids range over thousands of miles during their four- or five-year lifetimes, and all stubbornly persist in crossing, whatever the risks, the boundaries humans have devised. Migratory fish cannot be successfully confined as many other wildlife populations (if you landlock salmon, they become dwarfs), and effective protection is for that reason all the more difficult.

Because of this unique combination of strong consumer demand and the animal's sublime indifference to jurisdictional boundaries, the salmon fishery may be the most difficult of all to regulate effectively.

Add to this the complex legal milieu that has developed over the past 12 years as a result both of the federalization of fisheries law and a series of decisions in federal courts that protect Indian fishing rights. Stir in the staggering effects of habitat degradation caused by dams and logging practices, and you have in the Columbia basin what is probably the world's most complicated fishery management situation.

On September 14, 1805, not long after their first taste of Pacific salmon, Lewis and Clark camped on the banks of the Lochsa River, a small but spectacular river that rises just west of the Continental Divide in the Idaho panhandle (see map on pages 48-49).

The Lochsa is relatively far up the part of the Columbia River basin where salmon still run, and a fingerling that hatches in this river must travel through a representative sample of the structural obstacles and management jurisdictions that today characterize the Columbia basin. Thus, we have chosen a Lochsa River fish to represent the plight of all Pacific Northwest salmonids, and of the Columbia River itself.

A 19th century Lochsa River hatchling would have smoothly migrated downstream into the Clearwater, Snake, and Columbia before reaching the ocean. A four-year journey would have carried the juvenile fish thousands of miles northward into the Gulf of Alaska, perhaps as far as the Aleutian Islands, before it turned to begin its homeward journey.

A returning salmon migrating up the Columbia to spawn in the

Lochsa in 1805, when Lewis and Clark were rafting down the river, would have encountered a vigorous Indian fishery. The explorers, passing more than 100 stations where they observed Indians fishing, on October 22 reached Celilo Falls, 200 miles upstream from the mouth of the Columbia. Here was as grand a spectacle as the Columbia basin has ever offered, a place where Indians had been fishing for at least 9000 years. At Celilo Falls, Indian fishermen dipped their nets into the churning waters, where fish struggled to leap the height of the cataract with prodigious bursts of energy.

The aboriginal fishery Lewis and Clark saw was no mere cottage industry: the annual salmon harvest exceeded 18 million pounds. (In comparison, the 1980 total commercial catch of Columbia River salmon was 6.8 million pounds.) The Columbia River tribes were a mercantile people; bales of dried and pounded salmon jerky were a medium of exchange among inland tribes. Modern Indian court cases have been brought to preserve a small measure of that way of life.

The late 20th century Lochsa River salmon we are following faces obstacles far more lethal and implacable than Indians with spears and dipnets. The worst of these are dams. As recently as 30 years ago, a salmon bound for the gravel bar of its birth far up the Lochsa River had only two dams to cross — both equipped with fish ladders.

In 1956, the most difficult upstream obstacle was Celilo Falls, the site of the Indian fishery so vividly described by Lewis and Clark. At that time Indians still fished there by traditional methods. But a vital part of the heritage of the Pacific Northwest was about to disappear under 75 feet of water, as the gates of a new dam were closed at a settlement called The Dalles.

On a Sunday afternoon in April 1956, representatives of the fishing tribes gathered for the last time to hold their ceremonies on the bluffs overlooking the falls where years before Lewis and Clark had smoked a pipe of peace with their ancestors. Within one year, Celilo Falls, one of the last natural monuments of the river as Lewis and Clark knew it, was gone.

Today, the landscape of Washington, Oregon, and Idaho has been thoroughly reworked as a result of hydropower development. Hardly any major stream of the 260,000-square-mile Columbia River watershed has been left unaffected. The unobstructed Columbia of 1805, down which Lewis and Clark drifted with only a single portage at Celilo Falls, is today a stairstep series of slackwater reservoirs.

Only 50 miles of the 1214-mile-long section of river from the first dam up to the Canadian border now remain free-flowing. A once wild river that drains a land area larger than France and whose annual discharge into the ocean is more than twice that of the Nile has become meek and submissive — a series of back-to-back placid computer-regulated lakes.

Fifty years ago, there were no dams on the Columbia. As they had done for thousands of years, migrating salmonids deftly leapt the few natural obstacles. Today the main-stem Columbia has 11 dams; its principal tributary, the Snake, has 10. In the entire basin there are now 79 hydroelectric projects, each with a capacity of 15 megawatts or more. The Columbia-Snake is the most highly developed river system in the world, supplying more than 80 percent of the region's electrical energy.

Hydroelectric projects have been ruinous to the health of the salmon runs. The dams have permanently blocked fish access to vast regions of spawning habitat and inflicted high mortality on downstream migrating juveniles by obstructing passage. Because they have flooded spawning beds, altered flow patterns, and warmed water temperatures, less than half the spawning habitat available in the time of Lewis and Clark is now accessible to migratory fish, and much of what remains has been transformed into an environment hostile to fish propagation. Recent salmon harvests in the river have hovered around 10 percent of the historic highs of the 1880s.

A wild fish hatching in the Lochsa River must now accomplish the passage of eight dams, both in the downstream direction as a juvenile, and then in the upstream direction as an adult seeking its spawning stream. Juvenile fish mortality may approach 25 percent at each of the eight dams during periods of low river flow. In addition, a beleaguered wild hatchling must compete with hosts of its better-fed, and therefore larger, hatchery-bred cousins. The dams have exacted a far higher toll than anything else has, but competition from hatchery-bred fish is further reducing the number of wild survivors.

As the river has been tamed, so have the fish. In the early 1960s, Columbia basin states and the federal government joined to mount a massive campaign to rebuild salmon runs by increasing the output of artificially reared fish from hatcheries. As a result, only about 30 percent of the basin's salmonids today are wild fish, with the ratio rapidly declining. In 1981, the vast network of public and private hatcheries from California to Alaska released more than one billion salmon hatchlings, with ecological effects that are yet largely unknown.

This sudden expansion, rather than supplementing natural stocks, has itself been an important cause of further depletion of wild salmon runs. Leaving wild stocks to fend for themselves while tending to the needs of hatchery fish only makes wild fish more vulnerable to increased competition. Hatchery fish also tend to become inbred, displacing natural gene pools that have been responsible for thousands of years of successful adaptation.

This increased reliance on hatchery fish worries many practitioners of fishery science. Wildlife ecologist and philosopher Aldo Leopold 50 years ago contributed the fundamental insight that wildlife conservation is better accomplished by protecting animals' habitat than by interfering with the animals or their life cycles. Today, many see that habitat restoration is the preferred route to strengthening the salmon. Carefully planned stream improvement projects and adequate protection from overfishing will allow depleted fish runs to rebuild themselves.

One example of more or less natural enhancement would be to allow dams to spill water at times when juvenile fish need a steady flow of cold water to move them toward the ocean. The "water budget" program developed under the provisions of the Northwest Power Planning Act of 1980 provides a mechanism to do just that. The water budget is an attempt to deal with a critical problem appreciated only recently — the difficulty of balancing the water-flow needs of juvenile fish with power, irrigation, and flood control. The water budget allocates increased flows at those times of the year when downstream migration is highest. This approach gives fishery agencies partial control over the quantity and timing of river flow over the dams.

Despite recent advances in habitat enhancement, human-made hazards to the fish remain, and they are not only physical. As a result of legal and political events in the last 12 years, fishery managers must now untangle legal snarls and complex networks of responsibility that were undreamed of when Celilo Falls disappeared under the reservoir behind The Dalles Dam just over 30 years ago. Today's scientific, legal, and jurisdictional problems are nothing short of labyrinthine.

The wide-ranging migration of a Lochsa River chinook that now travels to the Gulf of Alaska and back will carry it through 17 separate

Oregon Historical Society

Fishermen at Celilo Falls, 1941, before it was inundated behind The Dalles Dam

management jurisdictions, each with some degree of independent authority to allocate the harvest of that fish. These include three international treaties that contain provisions on the harvest of Pacific salmon of North American origin, in addition to the authorities of one foreign nation (Canada), four state fish and wildlife agencies (Idaho, Washington, Oregon, and Alaska), one interstate compact, two regional fishing councils established by the 1976 Magnuson Act (which extended U.S. dominion over fisheries two hundred miles out), two federal agencies, and four Indian tribes. So a migrating Lochsa River salmon must survive not only hooks, nets, predators, and dams, but also a host of bureaucrats, interest groups, lawyers, and federal court judges.

The major laws necessary for the full protection of the Pacific Northwest's salmon resource are now in place. They include the Pacific Salmon Treaty between the United States and Canada, ratified in 1985, and the Northwest Power Planning Act of 1980, which for the first time mandates that the health of the Columbia River salmon fishery be given equal status with power generation.

But protection is not restoration, and full restoration requires enhancement of laws as well as habitat. Legal reforms of the past 12 years have themselves played a conspicuous role in multiplying management problems beyond the point of intelligibility. The very institutions designed to protect the resource have now, by virtue of their numbers and unwieldiness, become an additional threat. Like the sorcerer's apprentice of Goethe's fable, today's salmon managers are perhaps more in peril of being overwhelmed by the "solution" than by the original problem.

The chief obstacles to effective restoration are institutional in nature and international in scope. Any permanent solution must go to the heart both of our federalist system of shared power and of the intricate network of national sovereignties on which our world order is based. When an overexploited living resource respects no boundaries, the boundaries themselves must be treated in a way that respects the realities of nature.

At a minimum, full restoration of the Pacific salmon runs requires that the law be applied over the fish's entire migratory range, and that it be applied with consistency over the entire network of responsible management bodies. Otherwise, these magnificent wild salmon runs will remain caught in a trap the law itself has set — the creation of so many autonomous authorities that none by itself has sufficient incentive to conserve for fear that the fish will only be harvested elsewhere. It is the same "tragedy of the commons" that played itself out on public-domain grazing lands.

Harvested salmon

Many questions regarding the future of the Columbia salmon runs remain to be asked, and all will require answers before the turn of the century. Is it possible to restore riparian habitats in the Columbia basin to the point where the fish runs can regain the abundance of those legendary days when the resource perpetually renewed itself without the encumbrances of management plans, seasons, gear restrictions, quotas, and the politics of allocation? Do we possess the will to care for the watershed lands that nurture the rivers? Are we willing to harness diversions that suck water from the streams? Do we have the resolve to curb our appetite for still more dams? Or will wild salmon go the way of the buffalo, a curiosity protected on special preserves for sightseers, with the commercial market for salmon being met entirely by hatchery-raised fish — the equivalent, perhaps, of domestic cattle in feed lots?

We have come far in our commitment to bring the Columbia basin salmon runs up to their historic levels. To lose them now by default would be a major defeat, not only to those who depend upon them for a livelihood, but also to those now privileged to dine upon the incomparable flesh of upriver wild chinook, to feel their pulse at the end of a line, or simply to marvel at them as they leap over mountain waterfalls. Without these splendid creatures to lend their grace and beauty to the streams and rivers of the Pacific Northwest, many of us will indeed suffer from the great loneliness of spirit that Chief Seattle foretold.

Bibliographic Note

This chapter is an abbreviated version of Wilkinson and Conner, "The Law of the Pacific Salmon Fishery," in *Kansas Law Review,* vol. 32 (1983). A reprint is available free from Sea Grant Communications, Oregon State University, Corvallis, Oregon 97331. A general introduction to issues discussed in this chapter is Anthony Netboy's *The Columbia River Salmon and Steelhead Trout: Their Fight for Survival* (1980). A more popular work is Bruce Brown's *Mountain in the Clouds: A Search for the Wild Salmon* (1982). For a biological perspective, see the magnificently illustrated *Pacific Salmon* by R.J. Childerhose and Marj Trim (1979). For a detailed and highly readable history of the Columbia River salmon fishery from aboriginal times to the present, see Courtland Smith's *Salmon Fishers of the Columbia* (1979).

On the dams vs. fish dilemma, see Michael Blumm's article "Hydropower vs. Salmon," in *Environmental Law,* vol. 11 (1981), also available free from the Sea Grant office listed above. On Indian fishing rights decisions, see Jack Landau's article "Empty Victories" in *Environmental Law,* vol. 10 (1980). On the Magnuson Act, see *Federal Fisheries Management* (1985) by Jacobson, Conner and Tozer, available for $5.00 from Ocean & Coastal Law Center, University of Oregon, Eugene, Oregon 97403. For a detailed analysis of the Northwest Power Act, see "Promising a Process for Parity" by Blumm and Johnson in *Environmental Law,* vol. 11 (1981).

On the wildlife management philosophy of Aldo Leopold, see his *Game Management* (1933), *A Sand County Almanac* (1948), and *Thinking Like a Mountain* (1974) by Susan Flader.

8

The Dammed Columbia

Chuck Williams

The White men were many, and we could not hold our own
with them. We were like deer. They were like grizzly bears. We had
a small country. Their country was large. We were contented to let
things remain as the Great Spirit made them. They were not—and
would change the rivers if they did not suit them.

—Chief Joseph
(Hin-mah-too-yah-lat-keht)
Nez Perce leader

There is no question that the Columbia River basin fishery was
once the most productive in the world. There is no question,
either, that, in only a century, the numbers of salmon and
steelhead caught in the basin dropped precipitously. Fish cannery
operations disappeared, tribal fisheries were reduced to barely
enough to supply the salmon for Indian ceremonies, and angling
seasons were cut to next to nothing.

—Northwest Power
Planning Council

Idaho Power Company

Hells Canyon and dam on the Snake River, Idaho-Oregon border

The Columbia River is the lifeblood of the Pacific Northwest. It rises in the Canadian Rockies and meanders around the basin between the Rockies and the Cascade Range for 1243 miles, absorbing such tributaries as the Spokane and Snake rivers before finally breaking through the Cascades and entering the Pacific Ocean. (See map on pages 48–49.)

From its headwaters at Lake Columbia in British Columbia near the Alberta border, the Columbia flows north, 100 miles deeper into Canada, before making a 180-degree turn — the Big Bend. After flowing south through evergreen forests, the river crosses the border and enters the Channeled Scablands of eastern Washington. This scoured landscape is the result of a series of floods that swept across the mid-Columbia region following the collapse of huge ice dams during the most recent Ice Age.

After flowing west through deep lava ravines, the main-stem Columbia, blocked by the Cascade Range, turns south, providing a narrow ribbon of fertile soil. The Columbia then turns eastward to merge with the Yakima and Snake rivers before looping west into a deep, narrow slot through the Cascades and to the Pacific.

The Columbia's largest tributary, the 1038-mile-long Snake River, also begins in the Rockies, flowing south out of Yellowstone and Grand Teton national parks. The Snake then makes a large westward arc through the lava plateau of southern Idaho, eventually turning northward and entering mile-deep Hells Canyon where it meets the

Salmon, the "River of No Return." Just north of the Washington-Oregon border, the Snake heads west for more than 100 miles, finally joining the Columbia just as the main stem makes its last turn toward the sea and breaks out of the inland basin.

What created this curious path to the ocean? As the Cascade Range slowly rose, most Northwest rivers were cut off. The Columbia, however, with a flow many times that of today's river, captured other rivers and cut downward into the rising volcanic range. The result is the spectacular Columbia Gorge, the only sea-level passage through the Cascades between British Columbia and California. Within the 100-mile-long Gorge, the Columbia's shoreline changes from sagebrush desert to grasslands with oaks to lush rainforest as the annual precipitation increases from less than 10 inches to more than 100. Numerous waterfalls, including Multnomah Falls, the nation's second highest, drop over steep basalt cliffs into the Columbia.

After exiting from the Gorge, the river meanders slowly past Portland and through 100 miles of Douglas fir forest already amply supplied with water. The mouth of the Columbia is six miles wide, and its fresh water can be detected hundreds of miles out to sea.

This diverse, twisting river has supported two very different ways of life. Before Euro-Americans arrived and began remodeling the basin, the Columbia River's huge anadromous fish runs supported a large native population.

Chuck Williams

Columbia Gorge

The salmon and steelhead trout, which live off and help recycle the nutrients the river washes off the land into the ocean, supported a string of villages along the great waterway. In addition, many other people would seasonally move to the river to fish.

The preferred spots along the river were the rapids and waterfalls in the Columbia Gorge. The fish were easiest to catch there. Also, being low on the river, the salmon and steelhead caught in the Gorge were in much better shape than those that made it farther upstream. In part because of the exceptional fishing, the Columbia Gorge became the main trade mart in the prehistoric Northwest. It was also the transition between the canoe cultures of the coast and more nomadic tribes of the interior Columbia Plateau.

Lewis and Clark's voyage was followed by other explorers, fur traders, missionaries and then pioneer settlers. Beginning in the 1840s, a flood of American immigrants followed the Oregon Trail to the Columbia Gorge, and then floated down the treacherous river to settle in the Willamette Valley. As a result of pressures generated by this influx, a series of treaties were forced on the Indian tribes in the 1850s that opened more of the Columbia basin to settlement.

The treaties gave control of the region to the settlers, but the river maintained its central position. As in prehistoric times, the Columbia was the main transportation corridor between the coast and inland basin. Steamboats plied it upriver to Kettle Falls, near the Canadian border, until the 1880s, when railroads made boat travel obsolete. Just as steamboats replaced Indian canoes, so did non-Indian commercial fishing and canneries — beginning in earnest a century ago — take over from the Indians the best fishing places.

But the economic dominance of the salmon and steelhead runs was not to last. Despite their obvious importance, other economic activities, such as clearcutting along spawning streams, have prevailed over fish in the political arena.

More seriously, during the past half-century, the Columbia has been transformed from a free-flowing river into a chain of reservoirs. The river is now the world's biggest producer of electricity, and Lewiston, Idaho, is a seaport.

These achievements have come at the expense of the fish. Above Bonneville Dam, located at the upper end of tidal action, only one stretch of the Columbia in the United States, the Hanford Reach, remains free-flowing. Ironically, the efforts of the Corps of Engineers to inundate this last stretch behind the proposed Ben Franklin Dam have been thwarted in part due to opposition from the nuclear power industry. That industry dominates the economy of the area where the Columbia turns west in its last rush to the Pacific.

Scott Smith

Storm on the Snake River Plain, southern Idaho

In addition to attracting industrial growth, such as the energy-intensive aluminum plants that line the river, water projects in the basin have transformed a large part of the sagebrush desert between the Rockies and Cascades into irrigated farmlands. Many of the farms produce wheat that is barged down the Columbia. Irrigation uses water that could generate vast amounts of electricity. Irrigation also has wreaked havoc on such important spawning tributaries as the Yakima and Umatilla rivers. Withdrawals from such rivers as the Snake also hurt fisheries by raising the temperature of the remaining water.

Unlike the Colorado River, which has less than a tenth of the Columbia's water flow, over-allocation of water had not been a problem. But today, even the Columbia, the nation's second largest river system, can no longer meet all the demands on it.

Huge new irrigation withdrawals, such as the Columbia Basin Project in eastern Washington, have strong support in Congress. Railroads and recent presidential administrations have opposed the large subsidies that maintain this waterway; nevertheless, the Army Corps is beginning large locks at Bonneville Dam to increase river traffic. Upriver, tax and other recent laws have encouraged a rash of hydroelectric power applications on important spawning tributaries.

The federal Bonneville Power Administration (BPA), which distributes electricity generated by the Columbia, is trying to build a new powerline, Intertie, to southern California. The resulting power sales will require more water to flow through turbines. At the same time, Indian tribes and other fishing interests are trying to get more water spilled over dams to increase the survival chances of young fish migrating downstream. The rallying cry is: Smolts over volts!

Another conflict on the river comes from the federal government's choice of Hanford as one of three finalists for the nation's main nuclear waste dump. Hanford is on the Columbia, near its confluence with the Snake. The same federal government is simultaneously making a substantial financial commitment to restore anadromous fish to the depleted Yakima River.

Electric power and its industrial users, irrigated agriculture, barge traffic, and logging make up one economic grouping dependent on the Columbia and its tributaries. The economies clustered around the salmon and steelhead trout, wilderness areas, wild and scenic streams, and national parks make up another.

The fight over wilderness is done for the moment, but the national parks issue is hot, with the major debate in Congress centered on the Columbia Gorge and Hells Canyon — the 'Grand Canyons' of the Columbia and Snake rivers, respectively. The resolution of these conflicts will be another indicator of the direction the basin is heading.

9

Salmon: Continuity for a Culture

Cynthia D. Stowell

S almon! Venison! Roots! Berries! The old man rings a hand bell and calls out the Indian name for each food. The people, seated at tule mats on the floor of the longhouse, sample tiny portions of the sacred foods from their plates. When the old man calls "choosh!" everyone drinks a swallow of water and reaches family-style for the many platters of native and modern food. The feast ends with a prayer and another "choosh."

Every ceremonial feast on the Warm Springs Reservation in Oregon begins with salmon and ends with water. For the people, and for their ancestors along the Columbia River, salmon has long been the most treasured of foods, and water the purest. Together, they represent the constancy and the bounty of N'chi Wana, the great river that shaped the culture of the Columbia Plateau people (see map on pages 48–49).

The Warm Springs people now have to travel 100 miles to celebrate the arrival of the salmon at their traditional fishing grounds. But salmon is still at the heart of reservation rituals, from feasts honoring the roots, huckleberries and wild celery, to funerals, weddings, name-givings, memorial dinners, and important political meetings. And while history has driven a wedge between the river people and their

Cynthia Stowell

A root feast on the Warm Springs Reservation

ancestral home, the river still flows through their lives in significant ways.

For about 11,000 years before Lewis and Clark paddled down the Columbia River in 1805, native peoples lived continuously along its banks. Around the time of contact, the people of the middle Columbia — Sahaptin-speakers above the present city of The Dalles and the Chinookan-speaking Wascos and Wishrams downriver — lived in small villages of five to 10 families (see map). The Sahaptins and Wasco/Wishrams, though different in language and cultural emphasis, were bound together by their "Plateau" lifestyle, dictated by the rushing river and the semi-arid land around it. They lived in relative peace and prosperity.

Each spring, the lives of both peoples centered on the chinook salmon that were migrating upstream toward their spawning grounds. Standing on rocks over narrow river channels, fishermen aimed their spears, set traps or swept the current with long-poled nets, capturing scores of the silvery fish with the valued pink meat. On shore, the women butchered and filleted the fish, barbecuing some of it right away but hanging most of it to dry in the warm breezes. Sheaves of dried salmon were bundled up and stored away for winter use or for trade.

In the summer it was steelhead or other varieties of salmon, in the fall another run of chinook. The river also supplied plenty of sturgeon, lampreys, suckers, and smelt, as well as some shellfish. For six months out of the year, the Columbia demanded ceaseless toil from the people it fed, but the river people were paid over and over for their efforts. As long as the fishermen demonstrated the proper respect for the spirits of the river and of the salmon, they believed there would always be enough to eat.

The Sahaptins and Wasco/Wishrams did not just subsist on the river harvest. Salmon was their material wealth and they were skilled at marketing it. In fact, the mid-Columbia was the center of a vast trade network stretching from the Pacific coast to the Rocky Mountains. During huge summer gatherings, the fishermen traded their salmon for such desirables as animal skins, dried meat and vegetables, basketry, bows and arrows, decorative shells, and even slaves. Because of the steady stream of visitors, the people of the Columbia tended to be cosmopolitan, accustomed to change and new ideas.

The white newcomers proved to be more change than the people could accommodate. Settlers, too, knew the importance of the Columbia, and in a mere 50 years had cleared the riverbanks of virtually all native inhabitants. The river people to some extent weathered the Christianizing and civilizing pressures from white settlements at The Dalles and Walla Walla, the installation of "fish wheels" at their ancient sites, and the introduction of disease and alcohol. But when officials came to them in 1855 with pieces of paper that described new homes away from the Columbia, they recognized that life as they had known it for centuries was ending.

The four treaties made with the plateau tribes in June of 1855 contained much the same wording and intent. They ceded ancestral lands and reserved land far from the river at the Warm Springs and Umatilla reservations to the south, the Yakima Reservation to the north, and the Nez Perce Reservation in Idaho. Payment for the land was in the form of farm tools and supplies, reservation blacksmith shops and mills, food rations and salaries for government personnel. The displaced people were supposed to take up an agrarian life and stay out of the white settlers' hair.

Partly as a selling point, the treaties also included a few simple words reserving a right that the tribes exercise today—much to the chagrin of many a non-Indian: "The right of taking fish at all usual and accustomed stations, in common with citizens of the United States."

In the early years of the reservations, many families lived dual lives, camping and fishing on the Columbia in the summer when school let out, and wintering on the reservations. This practice was continually discouraged by federal government personnel, who insisted that the future of the tribes lay in education, entrepreneurism, private land ownership, and a new diet. But the superintendents could not guarantee that crops would survive the short growing season and marginal soil, or that tools and rations would arrive from the East on schedule. The people often went hungry awaiting the benefits of civilization.

Halfway into the 20th century, the Columbia was still an important source of food for the reservations, despite inroads into the supply of salmon and the changing pattern of life on the reservations. An overly enthusiastic non-Indian commercial fishery, particularly in the ocean, and the construction of dams on the main stem, were hastening a day the river people thought would never come, when the salmon would swim less plentifully into their nets. Still, the fishery at Celilo Falls endured in a manner little changed over the centuries.

Then, abruptly, it ended. In 1956, The Dalles Dam halted the cascading water, and the ancient fishing and camping sites were covered by still water. The people held what they thought would be their last salmon feast.

Arguing with the Army Corps of Engineers had been futile. The citizens of the Northwest wanted electricity, irrigation, and flood control, and the loss of a few fish and a picturesque Indian fishery was a small price to pay. The tribes took the monetary compensation ($15 million for the Yakima, $4 million each for the Warm Springs and Umatilla, and $2.8 million for the Nez Perce), knowing full well that their loss couldn't be translated into cash.

It was a difficult time for the tribal councils, which were accused by their fishermen constituents of selling them out. Three tribes decided to distribute the cash settlements to individual tribal members. But the Warm Springs council decided to keep the sum intact for future reservation development. It proved a wise decision.

The loss of the Celilo fishery had a note of finality about it, perhaps even more than the treaty-signing 100 years before. A door slammed on the past and the tribes were forced to consider a whole new future. By the 1950s, they were somewhat better equipped to face new options. The Indian Reorganization Act of 1934 had returned some political power and autonomy to Indian tribes nationwide, although days of readily available federal loans and grants for economic development were still 20 years away.

Those fishermen who saw no future on the reservations put aside their dipnets, bought gillnets and motorboats, and became commercial fishermen like the lower river non-Indians. They launched their boats into the main-stem Columbia from the various "in-lieu sites" that had been reserved by the government as dams gobbled up their fishing grounds. A number of families, particularly from among the Yakima tribe, made a modest-to-profitable living from the river.

A handful of Warm Springs fishermen chose this path, but their tribal council went in a very different direction. Depositing the Celilo settlement in the bank, they thought long and hard about what their reservation land and resources had to offer. Taking $100,000 from their savings, they hired a group at Oregon State College (now Oregon State University) to advise them on the reservation's natural potentials. The five-volume results of the 1960 OSU study, which are still used in planning today, pointed to the reservation's 300,000 acres of merchantable timber and the natural beauty of the land as possible sources of income.

Taking another $165,000 from their bank account, the tribal council bought back a piece of prime real estate along the Warm Springs River, where a non-Indian doctor had developed a spa featuring the hot mineral waters that bubbled out of the ground. That was the beginning of Kah-Nee-Ta Vacation Resort, a tribal enterprise that now includes a 144-room hotel, golf course, tennis courts, tipi village, cottages, and Olympic-size pool.

The people of Warm Springs, always a hospitable sort, nevertheless have felt ambivalent about encouraging tourism on their reservation. Without the full support of the community, Kah-Nee-Ta has not lived up to its profit-making potential, but continues to be a kind of showpiece to the non-Indian world. Instead of tourism, the real energy of the Warm Springs Confederated Tribes has gone into their wood-products business.

It began in 1967, when the tribes took out a loan to purchase the sawmill built at Warm Springs by non-Indians years before. As owner of both the raw material and the processing plant, the tribes could begin to map out a future that would guarantee jobs and a dependable supply of timber. Besides the 300 mill employees, the timber industry has created dozens of entrepreneurial opportunities in the reservation forest. In fact, many of those who might have been fishermen 35 years ago now find challenge and satisfaction working in the tall stands of ponderosa pine and Douglas fir.

Warm Springs has also capitalized on the rivers within and along its boundaries. Contracts negotiated with Portland General Electric in the 1950s and 1960s have resulted in substantial rental income from two dams on the Deschutes River. Quietly inserted in the Pelton Dam contract was a clause enabling the tribes to one day develop a hydroelectric plant at the Pelton re-regulating dam. Today, Warm Springs Power Enterprises produces electricity that it sells to private utilities at a profit.

Gone are the days when the people shuttled back and forth between the seasonal bounty of the Columbia River and a questionable existence on the reservation. But as the standard of living at

The White Man Wanted Bright Lights, the Indian Money

She grew up along the Columbia River, where her family had dozens of scaffolds at the Celilo fishing grounds. When she wasn't attending Catholic boarding school in The Dalles, young Ellen was with her people among the rocks and the rapids, learning from the men how to handle the huge nets and watching the women deftly butchering the catch.

"It was unusual for girls to fish," she said, "but I learned to dip the minute I was strong enough to hold the dip net." Butchering was definitely off-limits to children. "They didn't want our childish hands on the fish. We could practice on jacks and steelhead, but we couldn't hang them up with the women's salmon."

From her elders, Ellen learned the rhythms of the river and her culture. There were times to fish and times to leave the nets idle, times to offer prayers and times to be silent, times to work hard and times to celebrate. From her mother, Ellen also learned

the commercial end of fishing. While her father dreamed of finding gold and getting rich, her mother teamed up with a white man to operate a fish wheel, which scoops fish from the river into a chute. Taking the money she earned, she traveled by steamboat to Portland to buy enough supplies for a year. But the family's caches of dried salmon were their real wealth; they ate from their supplies through the winter or traded them to Indians from as far away as Montana for buckskin and meat.

Ellen was prepared to live out her adult life following the salmon runs of the Columbia, until history took a different turn.

The Dalles Dam eliminated the Celilo fishery as Ellen had known it. "The white man wanted brighter lights in his home and the Indians wanted money," she says. "That's the only reason that dam is there." Fortunately, her family has also fished actively along one of the Columbia River tributaries, at Sherar's Falls on the Deschutes River.

Warm Springs has improved, the people and their leaders have not forgotten the sacrifice that made it possible. Neither has Warm Springs put the Columbia River behind it as so much history and sentiment.

Warm Springs and the other treaty tribes still speak of the importance of the Columbia River to their survival. And they continue to negotiate doggedly for their place on the river, for rights that at times have seemed meaningless in the face of dwindling salmon runs.

In fact, Warm Springs has been a leader in resolving conflict on the Columbia among Indian, non-Indian, sports, and commercial fisheries. Excellent legal representation by Warm Springs attorneys

Cynthia Stowell

Ellen Heath fishing at Sherar's
Falls on the Deschutes River

It is there that Ellen has gone to fish for the last 30 years. The site is described in a petroglyph on a nearby rock wall.

From their scaffolds at Sherar's Ellen and her husband Walter routinely pulled 60-pound salmon out of the eddies while sport fishermen downstream looked on enviously. Ellen canned and dried some of the catch for her family, traded some and occasionally sold a fish for cash. Until Walter died in the 1970s, fishing was just a supplement to the income he made as a heavy equipment operator. After his death, Ellen came to depend increasingly on her catch, along with stipends from tribal committee work. Then, in 1984, Ellen had a massive stroke and had to put her net aside. What keeps her alive today are tribal pension and per capita payments that exist in large part because the Confederated Tribes banked their portion of the Army Corps of Engineers settlement for Celilo. So the Columbia River is still supporting Ellen Heath.

— *Cynthia D. Stowell*

helped bring about the landmark decision by U.S. District Court Judge Robert Belloni in *U.S. v. Oregon*. Belloni ruled in 1969 that the treaty tribes were "entitled to a fair share of the fish produced by the Columbia River system" and that the state could only regulate the Indian fishery for conservation purposes. The Belloni decision provided the foundation for a second landmark decision in *U.S. v. Washington* in 1974, when federal Judge George Boldt ruled that the treaties' "fishing in common" language should be interpreted as the right of Indians to catch up to 50 percent of the state's off-reservation catch.

While these decisions did much to cool the angry confronta-

An Indian Leader Puts His Faith in the Private Sector

The Wascos were once the most influential people along the Columbia River. Skilled fishermen and traders, the Wascos knew wealth and power because of the chinook salmon that seasonally swam upstream into their nets and traps.

On the Warm Springs Reservation in Central Oregon, the Wascos who descend from these river entrepreneurs have taken leadership roles in tribal business and government. One leader is Kenneth Smith, who was the Confederated Tribes' general manager for 12 years and then took his expertise to Washington, D.C., as Assistant Secretary of the Interior for Indian Affairs from 1981 to 1985.

He was raised by his grandparents on a reservation ranch, far from the Columbia River. Although the family journeyed to the river each September to meet the migrating fall chinook, their livelihood depended on the cattle back home. Smith grew up knowing the meaning of a hard day's work but his grandparents also taught him more than that. Uneducated themselves, they believed that education was the key to their people's future, and they pressed Ken to continue his schooling.

Smith's degree in accounting landed him a job in tribal administration where he was soon being groomed for management. By the time he was appointed general manager in 1969, tribal business was booming. Kah-Nee-Ta Resort had been launched, the sawmill was operating in the black, job opportunities had mushroomed and the reservation's standard of living was rising visibly. Smith guided the tribal corporation through the halcyon '70s.

By the time he was tapped by the Reagan administration, Smith was known for his commitment to tribal self-sufficiency through economic

tions – both on the river and in the courtrooms – that characterized the 1960s and 1970s, the treaty tribes still find themselves on the defensive. They are not a voting part of the Columbia River Compact, which sets commercial fishing seasons for Oregon and Washington. As a result, the Columbia River Inter-tribal Fish Commission, or CRITFC, established in 1977 to represent the treaty tribes, often challenges the Compact's decisions in court. At the same time, some fishermen with little patience for the slow workings of the judicial system continue to fight their battles right on the river.

In 1982, 19 Indian fishermen were charged with selling fish out of season to undercover federal and state agents. In the course of "salmon scam," nine fishermen were convicted in U.S. District Court and sentenced for up to five years in federal prison. Warm Springs quietly let its one convicted member report to prison in the summer of 1986,

Cynthia Stowell

Kenneth Smith

development. "To be really self-governing," he said while carrying out his D.C. duties, "tribes can't have their strings pulled by the federal government. I have to push and challenge them to realize that it's not the government's money they need. It's help in strengthening the capabilities of Indian governments."

Still, when Smith began trimming the Bureau of Indian Affairs budget, merging area offices and eliminating some Indian schools, even his supporters at Warm Springs were skeptical. "I think I had some of the councilmen scratching their heads a little bit when I was saying we had to rely more on the private sector for our financing," he said.

Smith has since joined the private sector himself, working as an economic-development consultant to Indian tribes, including his own.

— *Cynthia D. Stowell*

but on the day the sentences were to begin, the Yakima tribe challenged the federal convictions by pressing its own charges against five of its fishermen and keeping three of them in tribal custody for a time. Tribal charges were eventually dropped but Yakima support for its fishermen was clear.

The two tribes have different ways of asserting their treaty rights. Warm Springs likes to negotiate and forge compromises; Yakima is driven by moral arguments that often supersede legalities. The tribes are united, however, in their insistence that the Columbia River is essential to their — and the region's — well-being. The fishing tribes on the Columbia say they are not just user-groups out to get what they can from the river.

As aboriginal stewards of the salmon and the water of the Columbia, the treaty tribes say they have a privilege and a responsibility to see that these resources are used properly. They want to participate fully in planning and development along the Columbia, not just to assert treaty rights or to exercise their sovereign powers alongside the states, but also to ensure that the salmon survives.

"Salmon Scam" aside, there has been an unprecedented degree of cooperation among various river-users. Record low salmon and steelhead returns forced the parties to bring about regional solutions, such as the U.S.-Canada Pacific Salmon Intervention Treaty (1985) and mitigation efforts under the Northwest Regional Power Planning Act. This spirit of cooperation has been rewarded with improved returns of steelhead and salmon.

10

A Working Relationship

Chuck Williams

The infamous Pacific Northwest Fish Wars, pitting non-Indian fishermen against Indians and the United States against Canada, are fortunately waning. The Fish Wars came to a head in the late 1960s, when Northwest tribes that had reserved fishing rights in their treaties began to successfully exert those rights and when ocean fleets began to catch more and more Columbia River salmon. Many of the animosities remain, but cooperation is coming fast. As a result, fish runs for the most part are rapidly coming back.

In a series of treaties signed in 1855, many Northwest tribes gave up title to the vast majority of their lands. (See map on page 94). In exchange, they reserved the right to fish, hunt, gather roots and berries and continue other such traditional practices within the lands they gave up to the United States government. The states, however, continually tried to prevent tribal members from exercising those rights. Violence broke out repeatedly, especially in the Puget Sound area, between Indians trying to fish and non-Indians opposed to their fishing.

Finally, in cases generally referred to as the "Boldt" (*U.S. v. Washington* for western Washington) and "Belloni" (*U.S. v. Oregon* for the Columbia) decisions, the courts ruled that those tribes with reserved fishing rights are entitled to up to half of the fish returning to the tribes' "usual and accustomed" fishing sites — and that there was also a right to protection of fish habitat (for instance, half of nothing doesn't fulfill treaty rights).

In addition to the commercial fishing interests opposed to real-locations, fighting Indian fishing rights became a major cause for some conservation organizations such as the state affiliates of the National Wildlife Federation, which is composed primarily of hunters and fishermen. Meanwhile, fish runs were collapsing. As numerous observers noted, the various fishing interests seemed determined to fight to see who got the last fish.

The collapse of the Columbia River's once-bountiful salmon and steelhead runs had many causes. Dams blocked downstream passage of smolts trying to reach the sea, as well as adults fighting their way upstream to spawn. Clearcutting along streams caused erosion that destroyed spawning grounds. Poor agricultural practices also hurt spawning streams, and irrigation withdrawals took water needed by fish. Over-harvesting by non-Indians, first in the rivers and later in the sea, was already hurting runs by the turn of the century, but the decline was not obvious because fishermen just moved on to other species as the favored ones, especially summer chinook, were depleted.

In the late 1970s, the picture started to change. Having successfully reasserted their treaty rights, the tribes assumed an active role in fisheries' management and began to realize the importance of alliances with conservationists. Sport-fishing groups began to place far more emphasis on protecting fish runs and habitat then on who got to catch the remaining fish. Commercial river fishermen, such as Russ Bristow, president of the lower-river gillnetters' union, began to understand that upriver Indian fishing was not the major threat to their livelihoods. And finally, realizing that a very important renewable resource, the anadromous fish, was about to disappear because of "blind progress," a consensus formed in the Pacific Northwest to try to restore fish runs.

In 1977, the four Columbia River tribes with established treaty fishing rights — The Warm Springs, Yakimas, Umatillas, and Nez Perce — formed the Columbia River Inter-Tribal Fish Commission (CRITFC) to be the tribes' fish agency. CRITFC has formed good working relationships with most fish-related agencies and conservation groups, and its staff of biologists has become widely respected and effective advocates of increased fish runs. The formation of CRITFC and its Puget Sound/western Washington counterpart, the

Northwest Indians Fisheries Commission, set the stage for serious cooperation between feuding fishing groups.

One of the most important steps in restoring Columbia Basin fisheries was the passage of the Northwest Power Planning Act in 1980. Congress initially considered legislation to establish a Northwest power council to bail out Northwest power interests, which were suffering because of unwise decisions such as the WPPSS nuclear-plant fiasco. However, environmental groups and Indian tribes persuaded Congress to add important conservation measures, such as giving fish runs equal consideration with power generation in river-management decisions.

Among the successes of the Northwest Power Planning Act has been the Fish Passage Center (formerly called the Water Budget Center). It coordinates fish agency and tribal requests for increased flows when needed to help fish runs, such as spilling more water over dams so as to minimize the number of smolts killed by going through the turbines. Fifteen percent of the young fish heading downriver are killed by each dam, with total mortalities up to 95 percent in low-water years. Northwest Power Planning Council has ordered dam operators to achieve at least a 90 percent survival rate at all dams, a figure fish agencies and tribes are trying to get increased.

Another success due to increased cooperation has been the beginning of restoration of upriver runs. Congress passed the 1938 Mitchell Act to fund hatcheries to mitigate for damage done to natural runs by the many dams. Most of the hatcheries, however, were built below Bonneville Dam, in large part—as proven in documents obtained by CRITFC—to prevent Indians, who don't fish below Bonneville, from getting the fish. The result was that the upriver sports fishery was decimated along with the tribal fishery. Mandating the restoration of upriver runs will be part of the (hopefully) forthcoming settlement of the long-running *U.S. v. Oregon* suit.

Most tribal and sports fishing organizations prefer wild and naturally spawning fish to hatchery fish, which are vulnerable to diseases and budget cuts. Since non-hatchery runs require good spawning habitat, habitat protection has become the focus of much cooperation. In 1984, for example, the tribes, the Oregon Natural Resources Council, Audubon, Oregon Trout, and other environmental groups helped establish the 121,000-acre North Fork John Day Wilderness, the spawning grounds for the largest wild spring chinook run left in Oregon.

Protecting spawning habitat, something that benefits all fishing interests, provided an easy opening for cooperation. In a radical turnabout from previous decades, Warm Springs Indians now serve on the board of the Oregon Wildlife Federation, which also co-sponsors an annual conservation conference with the Warm Springs Tribe.

But a few groups still refuse to work with the tribes. In 1984, for example, the Washington State Sportsmen's Council, that state's Wildlife Federation affiliate, put considerable effort into passing Initiative 456 (a ballot measure to abrogate Indian treaty rights), all the while fighting Columbia Gorge protection and opposing wilderness legislation, even though both would protect spawning habitat.

The flip side of conservation/production is, of course, allocation of harvests. Here, too, much of the previous divisiveness is evaporating. Year after year until very recently, the states of Oregon and Washington tried to deny Indians their legal share of fish. And year after year the tribes would go to court to get their fair share. Now, thanks in large part to Bill Wilkerson, director of the Washington Department of Fisheries, and Jack Donaldson, retiring director of the Oregon Department of Fish and Wildlife, tribal seasons are set through negotiation, not litigation.

Oregon Historical Society, neg. #orhi 77408

Bonneville Dam and semi-circular fish ladders, which lead fish around the dam

Only the Idaho attorney general and Department of Fish and Game still prefer to settle disputes in court—and in 1986 even Idaho didn't file suit against treaty fishing of fall chinook and salmon.

The crowning piece of cooperation came in 1985, with the signing of the long-sought U.S.-Canada Pacific Salmon Treaty. Columbia River fish interests were increasingly frustrated because their efforts to increase fish runs were undermined by huge Alaskan and Canadian harvests while those fish were in the ocean. Meanwhile, U.S. fishermen were harvesting Canada's Fraser River stocks.

After almost two decades of fruitless attempts, the treaty became a reality because of a cooperative effort that would have been inconceivable only a few years earlier. Led by such unlikely allies as Mark Cedergreen of the Washington State Charter Boat Association, Jerry Pavletich of Trout Unlimited, and Tim Wapato of the Columbia River Inter-Tribal Fish Commission, the Pacific Salmon Treaty Coalition formed and convinced the interested parties to each give a little so that agreement could be reached. The Pacific Salmon Treaty—controls on ocean harvests—was the missing link needed to obtain "gravel to gravel," or life-cycle management of Columbia River salmon. Within a year, the Alaskan-Canadian catch of Columbia River fall chinook has dropped from 45 percent of the run to 35 percent—and is expected to drop to 25 percent next year.

Now most major components needed to restore Columbia River salmon and steelhead runs are in place. Although much work remains to be done, the results of the cooperative efforts of recent years are already evident in the fact of growing runs.

Unfortunately, all is not yet calm in the Columbia River Basin. Some fishing interests, especially in Idaho, seem bent on reigniting the 'fish wars' by trying to keep treaty Indians from getting their share of the runs and from being co-managers of Columbia River fisheries.

11

The View from the Upper Basin

Pat Ford

I daho salmon and steelhead are ocean-going fish. Born in mountain creeks and streams, they migrate up to 900 miles to the Pacific Ocean. They range widely in the ocean for one to four years, and then return – in a long, ferocious migration upstream – to their stream of birth to spawn. Most then die; each spring the cycle renews.

The Columbia River drainage historically supported the world's largest runs of chinook salmon and steelhead trout. Idaho's Salmon and Clearwater river drainages, high in the Columbia basin, are its largest intact nurseries for wild salmon and steelhead. (See map on pages 48–49.) Hundreds of thousands of adult salmon and steelhead plunge into Idaho and up its streams, from spring through fall, each year.

For many thousands of years, these overlapping runs of protein-rich fish supported major Native American fisheries and cultures in and around the present state of Idaho. In 1805, Lewis and Clark descended Lolo Pass and bought dried salmon from some Nez Perce Indians. Within 75 years, non-Indians were in control of settlement and development; in 1890, Idaho was a state. From that time to the

present, a series of blows devastated Idaho salmon and steelhead and those dependent on them.

Non-Indians quickly built intensive subsistence and commercial fisheries, in river and ocean, on seemingly inexhaustible runs. Over-fishing depleted the prized fish—big spring and summer chinooks returning to Idaho—and then shrank other runs as well. At the same time, habitat was steadily lost as settlement, irrigation, logging, grazing, and mining dewatered and dirtied streams.

Then came the greatest blows, the massive hydroelectric dam projects built on the Snake and Columbia rivers between 1938 and 1975. They inundated hundreds of miles of spawning habitat and migration corridors. Then in the 1960s, dams in Hells Canyon blocked all fish passage to the upper Snake River, entirely eliminating 50 percent of salmon and steelhead habitat in Idaho. (See map on page 94.)

The eight dams that are passable to fish, which form a gauntlet between Idaho and the ocean, claimed up to 15 percent of each run — both returning adults and migrating juveniles — at each dam year after year. Up to 90 percent of all Idaho migrating juveniles were killed in low-water years. Compensation in the form of artificial production in hatcheries and fish passage facilities either was not provided, did not work when built, or worked only slowly.

A collision was brewing. By the late 1950s, there were growing and apparently insatiable Indian and non-Indian sport and commercial fisheries on salmon and steelhead produced in Idaho, although only a small part of those fisheries were in Idaho itself. Major hatchery and passage efforts did not keep pace with the loss of habitat and staggering loss of fish. It is estimated that nearly 44 million salmon and steelhead worth $6.5 billion were lost to Northwest fisheries from 1960 to 1980.

The result of this widening gap between supply and demand was increasing conflict among fishermen competing for a dwindling resource, and the loss of major economies. Indians and non-Indians fought a destructive political struggle, which achieved national notoriety as the Columbia River Fish Wars. These wars diverted combatants and spectators alike from confronting the problems inexorably reducing the number of fish to be fought over.

In Idaho, non-Indian recreational suppliers were put out of business throughout central Idaho. Indian subsistence fishing was virtually stopped. Records aren't available earlier, but in 1975–1976, three central Idaho counties totalling 8000 people lost 122 jobs as a result of declining runs. And this was after the greatest declines had already occurred.

Blows to the runs and resulting conflicts were basin-wide. Idaho's special frustration was legal and political inability to affect decisions spelling life or death for Idaho fish. Idaho salmon and steelhead, and related Idaho economies, were devastated largely by downstream dams and fisheries that Idaho does not control. Idaho salmon, for instance, are fished under 16 separate state, federal, tribal, and foreign jurisdictions. Idaho controls one of those.

This legal morass led Congress to enact the Salmon and Steelhead Conservation and Enhancement Act of 1980 to establish coordinated management. But Idaho was not included in the new law. So in salmon and steelhead management in the Columbia basin, Idaho is at the end of the funnel.

Look at the Columbia River system through the eyes of the last fishermen — the Shoshone-Bannock tribal members. Before white set-

Wild salmon in a clear stream

tlement, they fished the upper Salmon River and its tributaries, and parts of the Snake River now dammed to salmon and steelhead. The 1868 Fort Bridger Treaty, which put them on the Fort Hall Reservation in southeast Idaho, recognized their right to traditional hunting and fishing.

Today these Shoshone-Bannock fishermen offer contrast on several counts. As they fish upper Salmon streams, 900 miles from the mouth of the Columbia, they have been preceded by ocean, non-Indian commercial, Oregon and Washington sport, Indian commercial, Indian ceremonial and subsistence, and Idaho sport fishermen. The Sho-Bans use only the traditional spear pole; their downstream counterparts use drift nets, gill nets, rod and reel, hook and snag — modern equipment they adopted after their traditional fishing spots were flooded or otherwise destroyed.

The bread and butter of the downstream fisheries are hatchery fish; the Sho-Bans' aim is wild fish. The downstream fishermen take hundreds of thousands of fish. The Sho-Bans, painfully but purposely, now take just a handful each year. The downstream fishermen have some legal voice in management and allocation. Until recently, the Sho-Bans had none.

After debating the right course for years, the Sho-Bans went to federal court in October 1985 to seek an equal voice in the Columbia basin salmon and steelhead fishery. Their motion was supported by Idaho and opposed by Washington and the Warm Springs, Yakima, Umatilla and Nez Perce tribes. The sides make clear that today's Columbia Basin fish conflicts are not exclusively between Indians and non-Indians. They are also between upstream and downstream.

In the Colorado and Missouri river basins, the upstream-downstream conflicts are mainly about water quantity. On the Columbia, they are about fish. But the conflicts are similar in the sense that positions are strongly held, are emotional, and at times the two sides seem to speak different languages. Words and agreements mean one thing downstream, another upstream. The courts are frequently consulted, and their major decisions run the rivers.

From the time in the 1800s when white fishermen began pushing Indians aside, there have been three related issues at the heart of Columbia River fish conflicts: representation, allocation, and management. All exist today.

Representation   There have been two modern phases of representation, or who makes the fishery decisions. The first, from the late 1800s to the 1970s, had non-Indians in charge. From the 1930s on, those non-Indians were energy, irrigation, and industrial interests rather than fishermen. The result was the devastation of the runs. Idaho's energy and irrigation interests were part of that ruling group. Idaho Indians, like the downstream tribes, were on the outside.

The second, current phase began when the Warm Springs, Yakima, Umatilla, and Nez Perce tribes forced judicial recognition of their treaty fishing rights. Non-Indians howled, and sought political redress; violent confrontations, fed by diminished fish runs, erupted. But the tribes' rights remained firm, and they began a slow climb toward co-management of the fisheries and river.

Recognition of those rights helped Idaho fishermen by breaking the stranglehold that energy and irrigation interests had on the Columbia and Snake river management. But it did not bring Idaho fishermen to the table where management and allocation were being decided. One observer says that in the 1970s, "Everybody else did to Idaho what Idaho and others did to the tribes earlier – shut them out."

The lower basin tribes' lawsuit – its shorthand title is *U.S. v. Oregon* – is now an institution. For roughly a decade most salmon and steelhead allocation decisions have been made under its umbrella. In 1983, when presiding Judge Walter Craig told the parties to begin negotiating a long-range management plan, Idaho sought entry to the case. Oregon, Washington and the lower basin tribes resisted. Judge Craig said no, but was reversed on appeal. Today, Idaho sits at the table with Oregon, Washington, the federal government, and the four tribes.

In October 1985, the Sho-Bans followed Idaho's path and asked to become the ninth party to *U.S. v. Oregon.* "Our purpose is to get more fish in Idaho," says Larry Echohawk, then the Sho-Ban's attorney. "The number of wild fish returning to the Salmon River basin isn't large enough for our traditional fishery.

"It is painful that there are so few our elders cannot pass on the fishing tradition. We need a voice in downstream management decisions. We didn't want conflict with the downstream tribes, so we've tried since 1977 to join the Columbia River Inter-Tribal Fish Commission. But they rejected us."

CRITFC, often called Inter-Tribe, was formed by the four treaty tribes in 1977. Its attorneys, biologists and publicists have made it an influential advocate on every aspect of salmon and steelhead management. CRITFC's tribes opposed the Sho-Ban intervention in *U.S. v. Oregon,* claiming its treaty rights are not on a par with their own.

"We took a chance," Echohawk says. "The federal court could have weakened our treaty right. The downriver tribes have gone right to the point of saying we don't have a treaty right."

However, in late July 1986, Judge Edward Leavy, who replaced deceased Judge Craig, admitted the Sho-Bans as intervenors in the case. The decision is not appealable. The Sho-Bans, who have had observer status at the long-range management negotiations Judge Craig had instituted, are now a partner in them. Negotiation sessions have occurred irregularly for three and a half years. Progress has been slow, with both sides saying difficult issues remain.

In the interim, downriver fishing allocations and seasons are generally set a year at a time by Oregon and Washington, often based on agreement with the treaty tribes. Idaho says it is not always fully involved in these decisions; the other parties say Idaho is involved.

Allocation, or who gets what fish when, is the most visible and emotional conflict. "Not enough fish — particularly wild fish — are getting back to Idaho," says Idaho Fish and Game Director Jerry Conley. "Too many are caught downstream."

The Sho-Bans agree. But CRITFC's Doug Dompier says, "The (CRITFC) tribes take far less fish than they have a right to. And wild fish numbers into Idaho are increasing each year."

In 1984, Idaho Fish and Game predicted an excellent Salmon River steelhead run; fishermen and their suppliers got ready. When the run didn't meet expectations, Fish and Game led an attack on the downriver tribes. It charged that the tribes' commercial gill-net fishery on fall chinook had taken far too many Idaho steelhead. The two species are in the river at the same time, leading to so-called incidental catches. Fish and Game's charges were amplified by editorials, with Idaho sportsmen and politicians calling for a law to make steelhead a national game fish, off-limits to commercial harvest.

The tribes replied that Fish and Game's own mistake caused the small steelhead run. They said Fish and Game had released diseased hatchery smolts two years earlier, causing the reduced run. They cited documents to support their counterattack.

Another cause of friction came in early 1985, when the tribes decided to increase their ceremonial and subsistence fishery on spring chinook from roughly 2000 to 3300. Idaho sought a conservation closure, contending the run was too small for such a take. The court denied the request, possibly because the tribes argued that the spring chinook run had almost doubled, from 50,000 to 90,000.

The year 1986 was quieter. The CRITFC tribes' 1986 ceremonial spring chinook catch was 8100. Fish and Game was unhappy, but didn't act. However, a draft 1986 fall chinook agreement made public that summer got things back into court. The Technical Advisory Committee (a broad-based group of biologists which provides information and best estimates to all parties) estimated the planned season could result in incidental catches of 43 to 50 percent of the steelhead run into the Clearwater River. So Fish and Game filed a court motion seeking to be a signatory to the fall chinook agreement. It was denied.

Each year there will undoubtedly be another string of disputes over particular fish runs. They will continue until the stalled long-range management negotiations succeed.

There have been a few agreements. The Nez Perce are the only Idaho tribe to belong to CRITFC. While the broader disputes have flared, the tribe and Fish and Game agreed in 1985 and 1986 on small tribal and sport fisheries on spring chinook returning to Idaho's Rapid River hatchery. "We have, by and large, been able to work out our differences in state," Conley says. "Even so, we have a difficult time understanding each other."

Management is where the arguments over wild fish and harvest reach the ground. Downstream fishermen and Idaho join together on water flow and fish passage issues to spar with the Corps of Engineers, the Bonneville Power Administration, and utilities. There are, however, two areas of dispute: the mixed-stock fishery, and the production issue of wild and hatchery fish.

On the main-stem Columbia, different species and different stocks of those species are in the river together. In August and

Jerry Conley   Larry Echohawk

September, large numbers of hatchery and natural-spawning fall chinook are in the river bound for Idaho. These are heavily fished in the tribes' commercial fishery from Bonneville to McNary dams. But large numbers of hatchery and wild steelhead bound for Idaho are also there. They are close in size to the fall chinook, and many are taken in the nets.

"The result is that the wild steelhead are fished at the same intensity as hatchery chinook and steelhead," Fish and Game's Conley argues. "Biologically, it doesn't matter much on hatchery fish, but the wild ones can't take that level of fishing. We are not getting enough back to Idaho."

Conley says changes in the tribes' fishery — more careful use of net sizes, better timing, moving some fishing above the Snake's juncture with the Columbia — would reduce the impact on wild steelhead while allowing a sizeable tribal catch.

The Sho-Bans concur, in their case for spring and summer chinook. "Our view of fishing is primarily religious," Echohawk says. "The wild fish are special to us. They have survived. Not that we have no interest in hatchery fish, but our priority is wild fish. Strangely enough, we get little sympathy for that from downriver tribes."

The downstream tribes have a different view. They say the state of Idaho, whose politics have a strong anti-conservation element, is only intent on rebuilding a sports fishery based on steelhead. They say Idaho is willing, and has even let, non-sports species and their habitats disappear, and let the Snake be dammed and blocked to fish. The tribes claim Idaho sheds crocodile tears over wild fish and genetic adaptation, but that it cares only about sports species, whether wild or hatchery.

CRITFC's Dompier says, "Our numbers show wild steelhead escapement to Idaho is going up. We are not taking undue numbers. This last year we gave up 60,000 steelhead we could have caught so escapement would be high. The mixed-stock fishery is already effi-

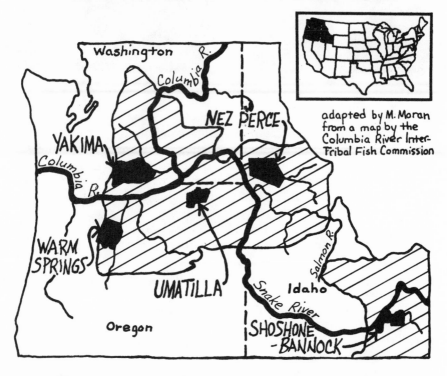

INDIAN LANDS OF THE NORTHWEST

adapted by M. Moran from a map by the Columbia River Inter-Tribal Fish Commission

■ reservation lands

▨ traditional Indian lands, ceded to the U.S. government

This map shows the reservation and ceded lands of the southeastern Idaho's Shoshone-Bannock Tribe, and the individual reservations and combined ceded lands of the four Columbia River Inter-Tribal Fish Commission tribes. Traditional fishing places of the five tribes extend throughout the Columbia River basin, both inside and outside the ceded lands.

ciently managed to protect the various stocks. We know exactly what's happening, and we shape our gear and timing accordingly."

He continues, "Idaho cannot rely on the 'wild' runs to rebuild themselves. We believe they should be rebuilt" by placing the right hatchery stocks into the streams. "That way, naturally spawning stocks can be built in all the unused habitat Idaho has now, We've got to do that rather than just continue dumping increasing millions of hatchery smolts out."

Conley counters, "Our program does call for rebuilding natural stocks in certain streams. We are moving slowly because it's difficult and risky. But there's no way we can outplant hatchery fish into vast areas of the Clearwater and Salmon; it's physically and economically impractical, and biologically dangerous. Those wild stocks in the Middle Fork of the Salmon or the Selway are adapted through thousands of years to do that job for us. We are committed not to lose that genetic flexibility."

'Outplants' are hatchery smolts placed in unused habitat (and Idaho has enormous amounts of unused habitat thanks to dams and pollution) in the hope that they will return there to spawn after their ocean journeys. If they do, a self-sustaining, naturally spawning population can establish itself. Presumably at some point established natural spawners can be called wild. There is precedent for outplanting. The best example in Idaho is the Clearwater River's 'wild' salmon, which were outplanted there 30 years ago.

The lines between hatchery, naturally spawning, and wild fish are vague, and their political use by all parties make them more slippery. To Idaho Fish and Game, the Clearwater salmon are wild; to CRITFC, they are natural spawners. Both accuse the other of over-reliance on hatchery fish and selective rhetorical use of 'wild' and 'natural spawners.'

Overlaying, perhaps determining, these biological and political arguments is economics. Columbia basin salmon and steelhead are enormous economic resources. Multimillion dollar commercial and recreational fisheries depend on the runs. Their low ebb in the late 1970s contributed substantially to regional unemployment. Their climb is sparking great economic expectations throughout central Idaho, as well as regionally.

Economics is a language our society understands well. For Idaho, when applied to salmon and steelhead, it is a powerful but double-edged sword. Fish can be compared directly, and favorably, with kilowatts and crops. As a result, political alliances among fishermen, businesspeople, and elected officials have been forged in the name of economic development.

Economics is quantitative, and the hatchery system fits into it more easily than do wild fish. The hatchery system represents an investment paid for by the nation's taxpayers. CRITFC's desire to use those hatcheries to restock a vast, empty habitat is economically efficient. Wild and hatchery fish are equally valued on balance sheets. The Sho-Bans' religious and cultural arguments make little economic sense. And many Idaho fishermen and their suppliers just want fish; it doesn't much matter whether those fish are born in the clear gravels of Loon Creek or in a tank at the Sawtooth hatchery.

Because more Idaho hatcheries will come on line in the next five years, with total annual production approaching 20 million by 1990, the prospects for continued rebuilding of Idaho runs are good. But the nature of the rebuilding remains uncertain. Will it be hatchery based, with natural habitats left in deteriorated condition or with healthy habitats left empty? Will hatchery fish be used to build naturally spawning stocks in now empty habitat? Will the wild stocks rebuild themselves? There is no agreement on the answers.

12

The Chainsaw Massacre

Hadley Roberts

For eons, the anadromous chinook salmon and steelhead trout have coexisted in the forested watersheds of the Northwest, which are important for the production of both timber and fish. Since the 1950s, however, when there was a large-scale increase in the demand for all resources, fish and tree production have clashed. In Idaho, for example, two rivers are being fought over, with loggers on one side and commercial and sport fishermen on the other.

The issue is the health of the fish habitat. Anadromous species reproduce in freshwater, and the juveniles spend time there before swimming toward the sea. To be productive, these spawning areas and nurseries must have cool, flowing water, clean gravel for spawning, clear water to allow sight feeding, invertebrate food organisms, lots of dissolved oxygen, and access to the sea. The lack of any of these qualities harms or dooms habitat for salmon and steelhead.

Logging can harm fish habitat in several ways. The fine material released by disturbed soils is washed into streams, where it settles on gravel beds and smothers fresh eggs. Other damage comes from the logging of streamside trees or the skidding of logs across streams. Both actions reduce stream stability and widen streams. The removal of streamside vegetation reduces fish cover and increases stream temperatures. Road building, an integral part of any logging operation, can be more devastating than the logging itself since roads contribute more sediment to streams than all other land-altering activities.

Examples abound of damage to salmon habitat by roading and logging. An infamous example occurred on Idaho's South Fork of the Salmon River in the Payette National Forest. The forest, made up of steep, highly erosive granitic soils of the Idaho batholith, was heavily roaded and logged from 1950 to 1966.

Toward the end of this period, severe storms in 1962, 1964, and 1965 accelerated erosion from the roads, and portions of the South Fork had sediment loads 350 percent higher than the pre-1950 period. The course-textured sands buried the newly constructed chinook salmon nests called redds under a blanket of mud, and fish that managed to hatch found the pools that past generations had used for food and shelter filled with sand.

Surveys substantiated the damage visible to the eye. In the mid-1950s, the South Fork attracted over 5000 returning chinook salmon and accounted for about 20 percent of the chinook salmon redds in Idaho. But in the years following the storms, the number of returning adults dropped drastically.

The devastation caused the Forest Service to put a moratorium on logging above the chinook spawning area and to start a watershed rehabilitation program. The action took the pressure off the South Fork and it began to cleanse itself naturally. By 1974, the sediment load was reduced 84 percent from its high point a decade earlier. However, from 1974 to 1983, the load remained constant, and it is impossible to predict when, or if, the river will return to pre-logging sediment loads.

With the memory of these grisly events only a few years old, a new controversy arose in 1981, when the Nez Perce National Forest proposed to log Meadow Creek, a chinook salmon spawning tributary of the Selway River. The agency's environmental assessment predicted a 20 percent decrease in the fishery due to the logging.

As a result, the Idaho State Department of Health and Welfare informed the Forest Service that its proposal was unacceptable. The agency said logging would injure a protected, beneficial use of the water — chinook salmon spawning. State standards say that no injury to beneficial use may occur.

The Forest Service and timber industry asked the state agency to relax its standards for water pollution from non-point sources, such as logging. The pair argued that enforcing the standard would eliminate many potential Idaho timber sales.

As a substitute for the state standard, the Forest Service and timber industry proposed the use of something called Best Management Practices. Under it, a sale could go forward, whatever the effects on water quality and fish, so long as the loggers used the best available technology.

After the Department of Health and Welfare rejected that proposal, industry turned to the Idaho Legislature in its 1986 session. Its HB No. 711 sailed through both houses of the Legislature in 12 days despite objections from 11 sportsmen's groups.

But Governor John Evans, reportedly under pressure from the federal Environmental Protection Agency, which warned that it would impose its own standards on Idaho's rivers, vetoed the bill. The governor said it "created more problems than it resolved."

That veto and the salmon it protected became issues in the last Idaho election campaign for the U.S. Senate. Incumbent Senator Steve Symms, who was challenged by Evans, ran a large advertisement reading:

"John Evans is again stamping out timber jobs." In small letters was the message: "Senator Steve Symms working effectively for Idaho timber jobs."

Symms was reelected.

13

Showing the West
the Way

Verne Huser

Almost from the moment of their creation, the Western states began to search for a way to deal with federal control of so much of the West's land and natural resources. Approaches ranged from aggressive: the Sagebrush Rebellion and former Interior Secretary James Watt, to cooperative: massive proposed land trades, such as Utah's Project Bold, and various federal-state oil shale and coal advisory committees.

Varied as they might appear, the approaches had one thing in common—they all failed. Now, however, a five-year-long experiment in Oregon, Washington, Idaho, and Montana holds the possibility of success. If it works, this multistate guidance of the federal presence could provide a model for other areas and resources.

The Northwest experiment aims at turning back the clock on the Columbia River by recovering lost natural values. Although no one talks of tearing down dams or of letting irrigated fields return to sagebrush, kilowatts are sacrificed to smolts, irrigation projects are modified to keep salmon out of apple orchards and wheatfields, and the region's energy policy is modified to minimize or eliminate new dams and power plants.

It is easy to take an elevated view of the experiment, and to wonder if it could help to resolve wilderness fights in southern Utah or forest planning fights in Montana and Idaho. But to those in the Northwest, the experiment is not academic. At stake are the electric bills of nine million people, recovery of the Columbia River salmon fishery, and the ways in which the region earns its collective living.

The Northwest's present economy rests on cheap, plentiful hydro-electric power. The low electric rates attracted the electric-hungry aluminum smelters and encouraged a way of life based on "living better electrically." The drive for cheap and plentiful electricity helped lead to the pushing aside of the rights of Native Americans, to laking-up almost every major stretch of river, and to the nation's largest, most disastrous nuclear power plant project.

Now, driven by higher electric rates, by conservation, by Native American victories in the Fish Wars, and by a new mandate from Congress, the Northwest is under pressure to change. The changes are being implemented through a unique attempt to give the Northwest states more power over the federal presence in the region.

Although the result of this effort to change the direction of the Columbia River basin will be determined by millions of residents scattered over four states and 260,000 square miles, at its center are two agencies: one federal and one composed of the four Northwest states.

The federal agency is the Bonneville Power Administration, or BPA, a $3 billion per year part of the Department of Energy. Its transmission lines collect 20,000 megawatts of power at federal dams for distribution to 54 electric co-ops, 37 towns and cities, 27 public utility districts, 17 industrial firms, nine investor-owned utilities, six federal agencies, and 14 customers outside the Northwest. It distrib-utes roughly half the power generated in the region and provides nearly 80 percent of the region's transmission capacity. When the Reagan administration recently proposed selling BPA, it priced it at $9 billion.

The marketing of electricity sounds benign, but there is potential for controversy. BPA once planned a transmission line through a national wildlife refuge, only to meet considerable opposition. So it simply built the line up to the preserve boundaries, presenting oppo-nents with a *fait accompli*. The effects of its energy policy are more far-reaching. BPA's decision in the 1970s that the Northwest's future depended on new power plants, rather than on conservation, led to WPPSS — the disastrous attempt to build five nuclear power plants.

BPA's policies in the environmentally aware Northwest created pressure for reform. At the same time, BPA itself wanted new powers

that could only be granted by Congress. These forces came together in
Congress to produce the 1980 Pacific Northwest Electric Power Planning and Conservation Act. The Act satisfied the various interests
enough to gain a majority, but some say it achieved consensus not just
through compromise but also through vagueness.

The heart of the Power Planning Act is authorization for Washington, Oregon, Idaho, and Montana to create the eight-person Pacific
Northwest Electric Power and Conservation Council. With BPA, it is a
key element in the Northwest's experiment in state-federal
cooperation.

The Act broadened BPA policies in two ways. First, it encouraged
conservation and efficiency, rather than power plant and dam construction. Second, through the Council, it gave consumers, state,
tribal and local government, and fish and wildlife agencies a strong
voice in the use of existing energy sources and the development of
new ones. The Act called for the protection of fish and wildlife,
including improvement of Columbia River basin spawning grounds
and habitat, and required that electric power revenues be used to
restore fish and wildlife values the hydroelectric projects had
destroyed.

The Council has initiated a number of programs for implementation by the BPA. They include model conservation standards in home
and office construction; the Water Budget to flush young salmon
through reservoirs; and the $46 million Yakima Basin Enhancement
Program, to bring salmon back to the Yakima Basin. (See map on pages
48–49.) Major salmon runs had been destroyed by diversion of Yakima
River water to irrigation, stranding smolt heading for the ocean, and
dewatering the river when adult salmon were running upstream to
spawn.

The Yakima program is being done in cooperation with the Bureau
of Reclamation, and if successful will develop more water for both
agriculture and fish. Yakima tribal fisheries official Bill Yallup says
the number of redds, or nests, has increased thirty-fold in the past
decade.

The financing of energy conservation and of salmon and wildlife
recovery programs comes directly or indirectly from electric energy
users through the BPA. The Water Budget, for example, indirectly
costs Northwest consumers between $54 and $74 million in electricity not generated because the water is released to move fish through
the reservoirs. The BPA is also committed to spend $200 million ($10
to $20 million a year) from its revenues to improve fish-passage
facilities such as screens and spillways at main-stem dams.

The Council has also undertaken a broader attempt to influence
BPA. It developed a 20-year energy plan in 1983 to guide BPA over the

Gladys Sufert, Oregon Historical Society, neg. #orhi77407

Fish wheel, which scoops up fish, in the Columbia River

long term. BPA agreed with 84 of the 96 specific conservation suggestions, but said the remaining dozen "faced serious impediment to implementation."

Those few words of jargon are part of a struggle that has been going on since the Council was formed. Giant BPA, with its 3000 employees, recognized that the 1980 Act was a mandate for change. BPA also recognized that the eight-person Council and its 42-person staff were instruments of the change. But BPA didn't conclude that it had to take orders from the tiny, youthful upstart. Instead, it saw the Council as running a public involvement process that would provide BPA with advice.

For its part, the Council recognized that issuing orders to BPA would lead to pitched battles and years of litigation. The result has been a complex dance, made up of both feuding and cooperation. Dulcy Mahar, the Council's information director, says:

"The rhetoric doesn't indicate the close day-to-day working relationship between BPA and the Council." In public, she says, the "creative tension" often results in friction. But privately, the two staffs cooperate.

Former Oregon Council member Roy Hemmingway has another view. "On the whole, BPA has protected itself as an institution more than it has furthered the regional interest." Mahar suggests that while BPA doesn't move fast enough for the Council, it moves a lot faster than it did before the Council was created.

The differences have spilled into court. The Seattle Master Builders sued in 1983, challenging the constitutionality of the Council, and BPA joined the suit. The Builders were provoked by the Council's attempt to impose an energy conservation code on BPA customers. Among the Master Builders' several allegations was a claim that the Council was unconstitutional because a state group was giving orders to a federal agency.

BPA, avoiding an open attempt to gut the Council, intervened in an interesting way. It said that, as it read the 1980 Act, the Council could not direct BPA, but only make suggestions. The BPA said that since the Act didn't tell BPA to take orders from the Council, there was no constitutional question. For their part, the Council and its tribal and environmental supporters argued that the Council could indeed give orders to the BPA, and that there was nothing unconstitutional about it.

On April 10, 1986, the Ninth Circuit Court of Appeals ruled that the Council was constitutional, and that there is no bar to a state-created regional body like the Council giving direction to a federal agency.

The BPA had threatened in the Master Builders' suit that the assumption of such powers by the Council would destroy the working relationship between the two bodies. But Kai Lee, a Washington member of the Council and a professor of political science at the University of Washington, disagreed.

Lee said Congress gave BPA strong powers in the Act, letting it acquire new sources of electric power, in addition to its long-standing right to market power from federal dams. BPA's ability to acquire new sources of power, Lee said, meant that the states gave up much of their traditional role in power planning.

In return, according to Lee, the Northwest got the four-state Council, and the Council got the authority to develop guidelines, checks and balances. According to Lee, BPA, in the Master Builders' suit, appeared to be trying to back away from that delicate balance between federal and state power hammered out in the Act.

If the Master Builders' suit was an attempt to shackle the Council, a suit filed by the National Wildlife Federation against the Federal Energy Regulatory Commission attempts to interpret the Council's powers more broadly. The NWF says the Council was created to do more than just oversee the BPA; it is asking the court to order FERC to also comply with the Council's fish and wildlife program.

The Council has joined the suit on the side of the NWF. If the NWF and Council position wins, the Council's fish and wildlife program for BPA would presumably also apply to the Corps and Bureau of Reclamation.

For the Northwest, these matters are all important. For the West in general, the most interesting question is: Has the Northwest approach worked well enough to consider spreading it far and wide? Bob Saxvik of Idaho, the new chairman of the Council, believes that the Act and the Council have "been a good national model for other regions to take a look at, whether" those regions are concerned with energy or "other shared resources."

Timothy Wapato, head of the Columbia River Inter-Tribal Fish Commission, says, thanks to the Act and Council, "the whole climate has changed dramatically." Chip Greening, a Portland attorney and public interest lobbyist, said in 1985 that, thanks to the Act: "Utilities could no longer ride roughshod over the public interest."

Part Three

The Missouri River: In Search of Destiny

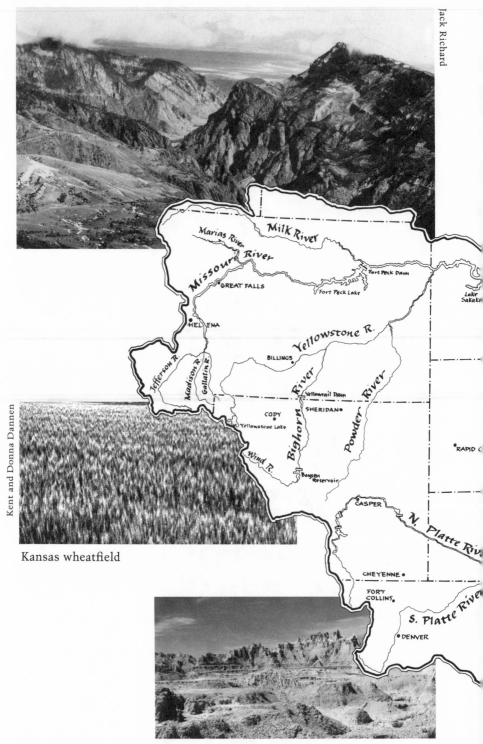

Kansas wheatfield

Badlands National Monument, South Dakota

MISSOURI RIVER BASIN

The Missouri River below Fort Randall Dam

Kent and Donna Dannen

MISSOURI RIVER BASIN

River Length (miles)	Basin Size (square miles)	Average Annual Runoff (acre-feet)	Average Flow at River Mouth (acre-feet)
2,315	530,000	61.5 million	52

Irrigated Land (acres)	Reservoir Storage — Active Capacity (acre-feet)	Hydropower Capacity (megawatts)
14.1 million	75 million	3,300

14

The Missouri River: Developed, but for What?

Ed Marston

The Missouri is America's longest river, and one of its widest and muddiest. It starts in Montana's Rockies as hundreds of mountain streams of the kind made familiar by beer commercials. These streams come together to form the Gallatin, Jefferson, and Madison rivers, and they then join to create the Missouri at Three Forks, between Butte and Bozeman. (See map on pages 108–109.)

From there the Missouri gropes its way north out of the mountains, emerging onto the plains near the city of Great Falls, and then carves a path for itself east across Montana — a state so wide it could easily be divided into two still very generous states. At the North Dakota line, the Missouri is joined by the Yellowstone, and the strengthened river then slants east and south down across the Dakotas and on into the lower basin states of Nebraska, Iowa, Kansas and Missouri.

Like the mountain and plains land that it drains, the Missouri's scale is hard to grasp. There is nothing puny about the Columbia or the Colorado, but the Missouri is almost as long as the two put together; the land mass the Missouri drains is larger than the Columbia and Colorado basins together.

Ron Selden

The Missouri River in the White Cliffs area near Big Sandy, Montana

The Missouri basin's runoff is dwarfed by that of the moist Columbia, but its annual flow is four times greater than that of the Colorado. As its Big Muddy nickname implies, the Missouri carries enormous amounts of silt. In the river's natural state, the silt caused the Missouri to wander back and forth across a broad flood-plain. The silt, when it settled out, created islands and built up channel beds, and the river would unpredictably relocate itself.

The Missouri also wanders on a larger scale. Unlike the other two major Western rivers, it is no regional stay-at-home. It moves eastward and southward across the continent to empty via the Mississippi, into the Atlantic.

Physically, the Missouri is a mature river. It has fought its wars with glaciers, which pushed it south; it has worked its way through soft and hard rock; it has created characteristic landscapes; and it has carried enormous volumes of mountain and plains soil toward its juncture with the Mississippi.

But politically and legally, and in terms of what the West calls "water development," the Missouri is decades behind the Columbia and Colorado. The use of its waters is not governed by a multistate treaty, or compact. There are few institutional arrangements among the states that share the river. Litigation over control and use of the river's water is just beginning. And although the Missouri would cause even a race of beavers to wonder if there is anything left to dam, relatively little of its water is diverted out of the riverbed.

Major economies have been built on the damming of the Columbia and on the diversion of Colorado River water to irrigate farmland and water cities. Now, other economies — the salmon, rafting, mountain wildlife, and fish — are challenging the singleminded pursuit of further damming and diversion that had dominated the Columbia and Colorado. In both basins, the choices between development and conservation are clear. Making those choices will be controversial and difficult, but the nature of the choices is plain.

The Missouri is different. The development of that river has physically changed both its upper and lower basins. But the resulting economies — hydropower out of the upper basin dams and barge traffic in the lower basin channels — have not been nearly as transforming as the hydropower, irrigation, and the building of desert cities that flow from the Columbia and Colorado. The upper Missouri dams have prevented some flood damage to downstream cities, but navigation benefits have been small. An Iowa professor calculated that transforming the Missouri through Iowa into a rock channel now yields that state only $5 million a year from barge traffic.

So the half-completed Pick-Sloan plan of the 1940s, which was to transform the Missouri River into the region's economic engine, did not create strong, new economies. But neither is the Army Corps of Engineers' dammed and channelized river being strongly challenged by conservation alternatives, as is occurring in the other basins.

Long dams block the Missouri's shallow valleys in eastern Montana and the Dakotas. Then, as if to compensate for the sprawling upper basin reservoirs, on the lower Missouri, especially on the Iowa-Nebraska part of the river, the once muddy, wandering, flooding river has been put in a straitjacket. Every inch is confined by rock or log walls to a narrow, swift-flowing barge channel.

Before the massive Pick-Sloan dams were built in the upper basin, the Big Muddy was a terror. It flooded the lower basin cities in high-runoff years, and left boats and barges in the river stranded during the low-flow summer. Today the large Pick-Sloan dams in Montana and the Dakotas hold back water at flood times and release enough water to float barges at low-water times. At all times the dams generate hydroelectric power.

A price has been paid for that navigable channel in Iowa and Nebraska. Gone, for each linear mile of channel, is a square mile of wetlands, oxbow lakes, meandering river, islands, and mudflats. Gone with them are most of the wildlife — the catfish, the ducks, the muskrats, the deer — that once occupied that environment.

Altogether, Iowa has lost 500,000 acres of wildlife habitat to channelization. A river that surged back and forth across a wide swath of land now stays in a narrow channel. The Missouri has been tidied, constrained. All through Iowa and Nebraska, the channel is bordered by farmland that occupies what had once been mud flats, marshes, islands, and riverbed.

Some lakes or marshes were left undrained and unfilled as the Army Corps of Engineers went about its riprapping, concrete-pouring, and wall-building. Now many of those lakes are drying up, losing their water to a dropping groundwater table.

The drying would be funny — a massive joke on the Corps — were it not doing so much damage to the surviving natural lands along the lower Missouri. The joke is that although the Corps locked the river in horizontally, it didn't pave the bottom of the channel.

The Missouri, as it emerges from the string of Pick-Sloan dams swift and free of the silt it once carried, is a hungry, down-cutting river. It runs down that straight, neat channel the Corps built like a power shovel, first dredging the channel (as the Corps planned) and then digging itself ever deeper into the ground. As the channel deepens (the phrase is "channel degradation"), the river drops. That, in turn, causes the groundwater level in the surrounding land to also drop, drying up surviving lakes and marshes.

It has been suggested that the lower Missouri be re-reclaimed in places. One Iowa state official interviewed in the 1982 TV documentary, *There Once Was a River Called Missouri*, suggested that the Corps stop maintaining the channel for barge traffic, and free the river to once again wander in its floodplain. The upper dams would still control floods in Iowa and Nebraska and generate electricity, but some of the river's natural values would be reclaimed in its lower stretches. The economic benefits could be large. A stretch of unchannelized Mississippi yields $1 billion a year from recreation and wildlife. If a freed Missouri yielded even a fraction of that, its value would be far greater than the barge traffic that now lightly plies the Missouri channel between Sioux City and Omaha.

The abandonment of barge traffic through Iowa and Nebraska might ease relations with the upper basin states. If there were no longer a need to use water out of the dams to float barges, the lower basin might be less quick to go to court when North or South Dakota tried to divert water out of their string of reservoirs.

Certainly the upper basin is owed something. The Dakotas and Montana lost the most beautiful part of their Missouri — the bottomland, with its fertile soils, easy irrigation, tree cover for cattle and wildlife, a varied landscape, and large fish. The Dakotas especially never got their share of the Pick-Sloan bargain. As originally envi-

Mike McClure

sioned, the project was to provide the Dakotas with extensive irrigation projects to replace the land flooded by dams and whose major
purpose was to stop flooding in the lower basin and to give them water
to float barges.

In an age of surplus Btus and kilowatts, of Gramm-Rudman-
Hollings, of massive farm surplus, of national hostility to irrigation
projects that cost $1 million a farm, traditional irrigation and hydro-
power approaches to the development of the upper Missouri River
seem antique. The West has entered an era of reform — the trailing
away of reclamation and the beginning of water marketing. But since
the Dakotas never went through an era of development, it is not clear
how, or if, they will adapt to the new reality.

As mentioned, the aborted development in the upper Missouri is
balanced by a lack of definition on the conservation side. The natural
and recreation alternatives to dams, irrigation and hydropower that
exist in the Columbia and Colorado basins, are not as visible in the
Missouri.

So Part Three on the Missouri River basin emphasizes basin over
river. The arid plains of the Dakotas are a neglected, little-known part
of America. Outsiders see them as flat, frigid, humid, blizzardy, and

boring. Unlike the mountains and the Western deserts, the Great Plains have not attracted preservationists and environmentalists, who inevitably act as promoters and publicizers of a region or area. The former Great American Desert is little known and little appreciated. But the land has a beauty, a history and a life unique to itself.

As a result of the incomplete Pick-Sloan plan, the entire basin became thin-skinned, and quick to quarrel. When, in the midst of the last energy boom, South Dakota tried to sell a dab of water to a coal slurry pipeline company whose acronym was ETSI, the downstream states sued to stop the sale. Long-standing attempts to build massive irrigation projects in the Dakotas to replace the flooded lands have also been fought and stopped or scaled back. In large part, the projects were stopped or scaled back because the Bureau of Reclamation couldn't figure out how to build projects that wouldn't do more damage than good to Dakota farming.

The Missouri is not all main stem. The Platte River comes out of Colorado and Wyoming to cross Nebraska (another candidate for division in two) and join the Missouri just below Omaha. The Yellowstone River flows northward out of the corner of Wyoming, through Montana, and into the Missouri on the Montana-North Dakota boundary.

One of the tributaries to the Yellowstone is Wyoming's Wind-Bighorn River, which is discussed in Chapters 18 and 19. Any small basin in the region could be used to illustrate how basins become

Bureau of Reclamation Photo by Glade Walker

Center-pivot irrigation machine

worlds unto themselves, binding those who live there together in cooperation and conflict. Along the Wind-Bighorn River, the story is of the struggle between Indians and white men over the control of the land and water.

The Indians had been steady losers in this struggle. But just as treaties give Indian tribes in the Columbia a right to a large share of the salmon, so do treaties in the Missouri and Colorado basins give reservation tribes a large share in the region's scarce water.

Where these so-called Winters rights apply, they grant the tribes enough water to irrigate their reservation lands. The legal principle is the same everywhere, but it plays itself out in different ways in different basins. In the Wind River basin, as Marjane Ambler describes in Chapters 18 and 19, a Winters rights victory by two Wyoming tribes has given them a bargaining position. Some of that strength may be used to get funds to rebuild and expand the Indians' deteriorating irrigation system.

15

There Are No Boring Landscapes

Peter Carrels

> I am not so sure that the prairies and plains, while less stunning at
> first sight, don't last longer, fill the senses fuller, preclude all the
> rest and make North America's characteristic landscape.
>
> *Walt Whitman, 1879*

I was born, raised and still live on the western prairie-northern plains and I acknowledge that Whitman was at least partially right. America's midsection at first sight is often less stunning than some of our continent's other regions. Even after a good long bit of watching, there are many who have difficulty appreciating the ecological and aesthetic significance of this "characteristic landscape." That troubles me for, like Whitman, I find the prairie and plains fill my senses fuller than other landscapes anywhere.

I suppose many form their opinions of our nation's grasslands as they chase vacations in their automobiles, an experience blighted by glass, speed and stereo tape-decks. Theirs is a non-intimate experience, part of a beeline to the mountains or coast.

Also altering impressions of my homeland is the constant manipulation of so much of the landscape. The business of food production has relentlessly tamed the prairie and plains, forever altering this chunk of America.

My part of the world has been easily subdued by man's simplest technologies. Access posed few problems. Virgin fields were broken with a single ox and a one-row plow. Formerly dominated by wild grasslands, it is a land now ruled by agriculture, much of it neatly organized into functional, food-producing units.

Eastern Dakota is a transition zone where the prairie meets the plains, where full-time farmers and full-time ranchers share trade centers. To the west is grazing country and herds of cattle and sheep. East is where glacier-deposited soils mat the land and the smell of earth under the plow fills the air.

Certainly there have been agricultural abuses. But just as we don't judge the significance of mountains by focusing on timber clearcuts or mines, so must we see beyond the impacts of exploitative agriculture to the natural beauty and bounty of the prairies and plains.

That beauty is easiest to see on hikes through surviving tracts of native grasses, vestiges of the grassland wilderness that once blanketed nearly a third of the United States. Last July a friend invited me to accompany him to such a place — one I had never visited before.

We reach the remnant prairie by crossing countryside that is flat and fertile, the bottom of what was a large inland sea formed when the ice of our region's last Pleistocene glacier melted and pooled in a wide, gentle bowl. Farmsteads are sprinkled about, their yard lights twinkling in early morning's violet darkness.

Far to the southeast a lightning storm rages, obscured by a veil of heavy clouds. Quick, bright flashes look like gesturing silhouettes behind nighttime living-room curtains. Occasionally a bolt is visible, sizzling and sharp, connecting with the earth.

Sunrise approaches and I am surrounded by spectacular dawning-day sky. My friend's farmyard is quiet. As we leave, the bright ball sneaks upward, then hovers, tubby on the sides, just above the horizon.

He points out our destination, a rise of land a dozen miles distant, the beginnings of the Missouri River coteau. The coteau is a terminal moraine that swells up dramatically in this flat land, its sweeping hillsides littered with glacial boulders. Farming is impractical on these slopes and land use shifts to livestock.

Local families have formed an association to oversee cattle grazing. Pastures are carefully managed to leave a sizeable expanse of land covered with unbroken soils. In effect, the local farmers have duplicated the grazing patterns of bison herds that long ago nourished themselves on the same succulent native grasses.

Western grebe

We wade through thick, healthy vegetation. This is a mixed grass prairie, where the tall grasses of the humid eastern prairie merge with the shorter grasses of the semi-arid plains. My friend listens for a Baird's sparrow, a bird becoming increasingly rare as prairies are plowed under. He glimpsed a Baird's up here before.

On top of the coteau the terrain is rolling and grass-covered. We have walked about for some time, and the sun has climbed a noticeable length into the sky; we are now completely surrounded by native grasslands. The depressions in this hummocky landscape contain sparkling marshes and small lakes or prairie potholes. The potholes are magnets to wildlife; we too are drawn nearer, descending a long, gradual slope toward a tall stand of canary grass that fringes the open water.

Our presence is no secret. A bittern flushes and wings off to a more private corner of the slough. Paddling blue-winged teal hurry toward a maze of high reeds. A mother grebe with two youngsters riding on her back retreats into a cluster of rushes. On the opposite shore two night herons stand motionless, and a couple of great blues drop from graceful flight, lighting in the shallows. A killdeer cries out its name.

Although agriculture has destroyed many prairie potholes in recent years, these wildlife meccas still pocket the northern plains. Wildlife scientists call the prairie pothole region "America's duck factory," for nearly 90 percent of all ducks that breed in the continental United States do so in these small bodies of water nestled among the grasslands.

Above the wetlands are the varied grasses: the bluestems, needlegrasses, wheatgrass, wild rye, Indian grass, buffalo grass, and a dozen others in varied shades of green. Winds sway the grasses, creating patterns that make the hillsides and coteau pulse with life. Children in wooded areas sometimes think trees make wind; here they think it is made by the grasses.

There are more wildflowers than you would believe. Wave after wave of them in native prairie. Pasqueflowers, small, delicate and purple, South Dakota's state flower, are a harbinger of spring on the northern plains. There are coneflowers, sunflowers, thistle, anemone, red blazing star, and many more. The prodigious growth is powered by the rich soils of the prairies and plains. A square meter of prairie sod may contain 5 miles of roots.

The prairie and plains are a sprawling, mostly people-less place. To some this open space is disconcerting and uncomfortable. I love the dome of sky and floor of land stretching forever, without landmarks, without scale. It is a landscape for dreaming and contemplation. It encourages looking inward as well as outward, not unlike the sea, with a smooth surface that soothes those weary from looking at too much.

Peter Carrels

Grain elevator

The weather of the plains is robust and unpredictable. In this country, all eyes turn to the sky countless times a day. Though there are practical reasons for vigilance, sky-watching is also one of the region's great pleasures. The sky here provides magnificent theater in the round. A massive weather-front laden with swirling, swelling black thunderheads, stretching to opposite horizons, is at once menacing and exhilarating.

I stand in an open field and watch the clouds approach. Bright flashes of lightning suddenly thrust from the darkening blue-charcoal sky, followed by exploding, crackling thunder that makes me flinch and shiver. I continue to survey the storm, looking closely for funnel clouds. Never mind that there appear to be none in this particular system, it is still time to retreat before driving rain or stinging hail arrive.

In winter we observe approaching blizzards. Like thunderstorms, blizzards roll in from the west, producing turbulent, chaotic rumblings, whining winds, and a shrouding mass of whiteness.

Or I watch billowing cumulus clouds building higher and higher. Or a yellow harvest moon hanging like a lantern in a large, empty room.

The sky is graced by raptors, constantly scanning the terrain for gophers, squirrels and rabbits. A meadowlark's melodic song rises sweetly above the breeze. Ring-necked pheasants hustle across a gravel road bound for uncut cover. Prairie chickens celebrate the mating season with flamboyant ritual. Males gather at display grounds to strut and "boom," hoping their bravado will impress a female audience.

On the high plains, pronghorn antelope race over the grasslands at breakneck speeds. They are America's fastest mammal. But gone are the legendary bison herds that once shared the range with the antelope. Only remnant herds roam the confines of national parks. Toward dusk comes a song-dog chorus. Coyotes, long common on the wild plains, are now denizens of the more populated prairie as well. They are the region's symbolic survivor.

Man also survives on scattered farms and ranches, and in tiny, isolated towns that serve those farms and ranches.

The skylines of America's towns give you an indication of where that community is located. What would a New England town be without a white church steeple towering above the rest of the buildings?

Travel west from the wooded hills of New England more than 1000 miles to the immense, semi-arid plains. Look at a typical town and note its skyline. Instead of a steeple, a water tower or grain elevators dominate the view. And in churches below, topics that sustain most of

Peter Carrels

The skyline of Roslyn, South Dakota, on mixed grass prairie 50 miles east of Aberdeen

Sunday's conversations are moisture — whether too much or too little — livestock or crop prices.

In this region, it is man's quest for more reliable water supplies and larger crop yields that fuels efforts to subdue nature. Irrigation interests promote river modification projects. Prairie potholes are drained to accommodate more cropland. Non-farm corporations and farmers alike point powerful tractors pulling huge implements at native grasslands. Vulnerable topsoils are abused and are then stolen by strong winds and hard rains. Stewardship is overlooked, side-stepped, and the natural heritage of this "characteristic landscape" is disregarded.

16

"The Most Useless River There Is"

Peter Carrels

T he northern plains is this nation's region of last resort. It was the region most recently settled, and it is the least appreciated, least understood section of the country.

America's northern plains occupy central and eastern Montana and most of both Dakotas, representing about 13 percent of the land in the lower 48 states. This is remote country. It is agricultural, with pockets of coal mining and oil development. The Badlands and Black Hills in the Dakotas, several mountain ranges in eastern Montana, and sentinel buttes in the middle chunk of the region are the only land forms to interrupt the flat or rolling grasslands or croplands that everywhere else dominate the landscape. And, of course, there is the region's river of legend, the longest river in the nation, the Missouri River.

Although the Missouri River is the seam that ties the region together, hardship and hard times bind the residents of this land. Natural conditions have long been seen as obstacles to the region's progress in traditional white-American terms. So, many of the region's political powers look to man-made water projects, using the massive upper Missouri River reservoir chain, as one way to overcome nature and break through to economic prosperity.

Peter Carrels

Trees inundated by Lake Oahe, South Dakota

To the earliest white settlers journeying westward, the northern plains was a bleak, intimidating land. They had come from heavily timbered states east of the Mississippi River to find themselves surrounded by endless, treeless, semi-arid grasslands, often lacking even the comfort of a distant promontory landmark. Snarling blizzards made for a miserable winter in a cramped, poorly heated settler's shanty.

In the eastern states, moisture came as needed and crops rarely withered in the field. For a settler accustomed to broadleaf trees and rainfall, the northern plains held no promise, no topographical or climatic lure. So they hurried through, to the bounty beyond.

The settlers had been warned of the "Great American Desert" long before setting foot in the open country. In 1855, Jefferson Davis had informed the United States Congress that the soils of the territory were sterile. Fourteen years later, Ohio Congressman James Ashley declared Dakota Territory a worthless land. Writers of the day vividly described the lifeless "leagues of desert" that had to be crossed on the way to the mountains and the Montana gold mines.

It was the swelling populations of mid-19th century mining camps that led to efforts at permanent settlement. During the first years of mining, food came from Mormon fields in Utah. The difficult winter of 1864–1865 saw the price of flour jump to $120 and more for a

100-pound sack—a $100 increase. Violence erupted between merchants and miners. Local sources of food were needed and some prospectors turned to farming. They applied their knowledge of sluice construction to agriculture, and simple irrigation systems soon fed the crops. They followed tillage methods used by the Mormons.

By the 1890s, the notion of the northern plains as a sterile desert was being proven wrong. Interest in the northern plains and in the West generally was buoyed by the census of 1890, which concluded that the "frontier" no longer existed. The nation had reached the coast, and now it turned its attention back to the vast 'pocket' it had skipped. Land prices rose and speculators went to work.

In what is now southeastern South Dakota, rail connections to Eastern markets opened the door to farm development; thanks to fertile soils and greater precipitation than in the rest of the region, settlement quickly expanded.

From east to west the character of the northern plains changes greatly. The east is where the tallgrass prairie meets the plains, and where crop-growing conditions are best. Nearing the Missouri River and west to the Rockies, most of the land is better suited for grazing livestock, with crop-raising concentrated in valleys.

Early promoters of the northern plains saw that the region's future hinged on its capacity to support agriculture. Just what sort of agriculture should be pursued was and remains a pressing and controversial issue.

Regular droughts ruined crops and tempered the influx of settlement. A prolonged dry spell was often followed by a drastic loss of population.

To counter drought, agricultural innovators emerged with ideas and schemes. Central to these ideas was the understanding that occasional moisture shortages were natural in the region. Two basic approaches evolved: dry farming and irrigation.

Dry farming does not mean farming without moisture. It means conserving the scant moisture. Agricultural experts say an annual minimum of 10 inches is required to dry farm.

Dry-land farming techniques gained fame by the turn of the century and rode a wave of popularity into the 1920s. Much of its success is attributed to Hardy Webster Campbell, called the greatest evangelist of dry farming by Plains historian Walter Prescott Webb. Campbell was a New Englander who moved to what is now eastern South Dakota in 1879. He had a distinct advantage over many of his northern plains farming counterparts: He had never farmed, and had no preconceptions. Also he didn't hold to the foolish adage plains settlers brought with them that "rains would follow the plow."

Campbell believed farmers must adjust to their environment. "Don't try to change nature's laws to fit your notions and habits," he advised. "Change your notions and habits to conform with nature's ways." To Campbell, the lack of moisture on the plains need not be fatal. "It is a matter of common knowledge that the soil of this region is of a texture admirably adapted to the best farming. The fact of the small precipitation has been the sole reason for the failure to develop the region," he said.

Soil stewardship was the cornerstone of Campbell's dry-land farming system, with croplands managed to retain fertility and moisture. When his yields dramatically outpaced those of his neighbors, Campbell's reputation grew, and soon he was publishing books and managing experimental farms for the railroads.

The success of dry farming was seized on by the railroads and other commercial interests to convince reluctant settlers that the plains could be homesteaded. And though permanent lessons were learned from dry farming, the movement became, more than anything else, a promotional tool.

Dry-land techniques were not the only ones used to settle the droughty plains. When it was realized that rain would not automatically follow the plow, the Congress authorized rainmaking research during the early 1890s. An 1891 bill in the North Dakota Legislature proposed a reward to anyone devising a rainmaking system. So "rainmakers" roamed the countryside, charging high fees to detonate explosives. The explosives, of course, created nothing but noise, and interest in rainmaking waned. But the desire to find a reliable source of moisture persisted. Inevitably, attention turned to irrigation.

John Wesley Powell had begun the clamor for irrigation projects in the region in 1878. Powell believed irrigation was absolutely necessary, though he viewed it as a way to supplement agriculture, not dominate it. In an early proposal he advocated granting 2500-acre homesteads west of the 100th meridian, with 20-acre irrigated plots for each homestead. The large acreage would be dry-land farmed. The irrigated plots would provide animal food and seed to carry through periods of drought.

Eastern politicians had trouble understanding the need for such immense homesteads. But Powell knew that the risks of plains agriculture necessitated large individual farm unit acreages. He also understood the need to create surface water storage reservoirs to facilitate irrigation development.

The first push toward irrigation development in the region came from a severe drought. The year 1890 delivered a brutally dry spring and summer. By 1892 Montanans were pressing their state government for irrigation development aid. Eight years later, federal aid for reservoir construction was aggressively sought.

The early debates regarding large-scale irrigation development and government assistance for these projects were as bitter and diverse as those today. And they had some of the same causes as today, for simultaneous with the interest in federal irrigation projects came wheat overproduction. Crop prices tumbled, and Eastern politicians complained that federally subsidized projects in the West would hurt farmers in the older states. They also contended it was unconstitutional to apply federal funds to serve sectional interests. And some northern plains leaders, particularly in the Dakotas, were reluctant to seek irrigation help for fear their localities would be perceived as "dry" by the rest of the nation.

But overproduction was overtaken by the prospect of future food shortages, and Western leaders began touting the idea that reclamation by irrigation was in the national interest. Eventually, both major political parties endorsed national aid for Western irrigation. In June 1902 Congress passed the Newlands Reclamation Act, a law that expressed the nation's twin beliefs that agricultural expansion was necessary, and that the semi-arid lands were capable of consistently producing crops only if large-scale irrigation projects were built.

President Theodore Roosevelt was given much credit for passage of the Reclamation Act. He was the country's first president with any experience in the West, having ranched in western North Dakota and hunted in the Rocky Mountains. In a 1901 speech to Congress, Roosevelt said, "It is as right for the national government to make the streams and rivers of the arid region useful by engineering works for water storage as to make useful the rivers and harbors of the humid region by engineering works of another kind."

But northern plains farmers were not so pleased by the new law. Many farmers were happy with dry-land techniques or with small irrigation projects. Businessmen and politicians, however, heartily promoted large-scale irrigation. In 1903, an enthusiastic three-day conference of Minneapolis, St. Paul, and Duluth business interests was held to support irrigation development on the northern plains. They welcomed the promise of a construction boom to be followed by drought-proof agriculture.

A 1904 plan to irrigate 20,000 acres in western North Dakota was promoted by bankers, commercial clubs, and area newspapers, and two years later, a large proportion of area landowners had been persuaded to sign irrigation contracts. But when the project was built and the water delivered, it proved so expensive farmers refused to use it.

Early irrigation interest in South Dakota was largely confined to the bottomlands along creeks and rivers in the extreme western part of the state. With the Reclamation Act came study and construction of a reservoir on the Belle Fourche River in 1908. Five hundred miles of canals were built as part of a plan to irrigate 90,000 acres.

But the project was plagued by mistakes, among them a fatal Bureau of Reclamation error regarding soil classification. It was discovered that almost half the project area contained heavy gumbo soils not suitable for irrigation. By 1946, only two of the original 580 homesteaders associated with the Belle Fourche Project remained on the project.

The failure of early large-scale irrigation projects in the Dakotas and the isolated, oasis-like pockets of irrigation agriculture that survived kept interest in irrigation mild. Between 1920 and 1930, irrigated acreage diminished throughout the entire region. There was no noteworthy public support for large-scale irrigation projects until smothering dust storms and drought ravaged the region in the 1930s. The hot winds of the 1930s blew farmers off the land and set the stage

Lyle Axthelm, BuRec

Oahe Dam, South Dakota

for the 1944 adoption of the Pick-Sloan plan, an ambitious scheme to harness the entire Missouri River basin.

Pick-Sloan's planners had the best of intentions. Their hopes were to stop destructive flooding in downriver cities such as Omaha, Kansas City and St. Louis, allow barge navigation as far north as Sioux City, Iowa, and enrich the northern plains with irrigation agriculture and hydroelectricity.

Under the U.S. Army Corp of Engineers and the Bureau of Reclamation, the Pick-Sloan plan did bring predictability to the Missouri River. By 1967, six massive, earth-rolled dams plugged the river's channel in the Dakotas and Montana. (See map on pages 108–109.) What had been the grandest, wildest plains-prairie river in the world was reduced to a series of mundane, lengthy reservoirs. Today, little of the natural Missouri River remains on the northern plains.

Pick-Sloan efforts to harness the Missouri River were extolled across the nation. "A technological triumph that overshadows the Panama Canal," wrote one magazine correspondent. But tragedy accompanied the triumph. Well over a million acres of fertile bottomlands drowned beneath the big main-stem reservoirs. Lush, verdant coulees and draws running up the river's valley walls were buried. A winding channel with gravel bars and chutes, lined with great groves of cottonwoods, was gone forever. What had been the most diverse ecological community on the northern plains was swallowed up.

Those who settled the river's valley also lost. Thousands of Native Americans were forced to relocate to modern tract towns. Entire communities had to be abandoned.

What is amazing was the lack of organized opposition to Pick-Sloan's Missouri River dams. It was a quiet tragedy. No major environmental group fought the dams. Some Dakota farmers protested, claiming irrigation from Missouri River waters would damage the region's fragile soils. But the protests were not heard. Nationwide, Pick-Sloan was praised. A September 1952 *Time* magazine story covering the Missouri River and Pick-Sloan's accomplishments described the Missouri River as "the most useless river there is."

Most residents of the region also applauded Pick-Sloan. They eagerly awaited the fruits of the reservoirs: irrigation projects. And downriver, city dwellers in floodplains breathed easier. No more would Big Muddy have its way with them.

Powell's dream of irrigating the northern plains from reservoirs was now possible on a large scale. The Bureau of Reclamation was prepared to undertake construction of two major irrigation diversion projects. Numerous smaller projects, utilizing stored water behind dams on tributaries, were planned as well. Over five million acres were to be irrigated, more than replacing the one million drowned acres.

The Missouri-Souris Diversion Unit was initially proposed to irrigate 1 million acres in the northwestern corner of North Dakota, but soil surveys revealed that dense, poorly drained glacial subsoils dominated the area. So the Bureau found another million acres in eastern North Dakota and renamed the project Garrison Diversion.

Behind South Dakota's Oahe (pronounced a-WA-he) Dam sits a burly reservoir called Lake Oahe. The Oahe Diversion Unit, the second of the two major Bureau irrigation projects in Pick-Sloan, was to take water from Lake Oahe by canal 100 miles east to the James River Valley. A 1200-mile network of smaller canals would then water 495,000 acres.

This time there was opposition, and the controversy, starting in the early 1970s, commanded headlines in the state's newspapers for over a decade. Most of the state's politicians, including two different governors and the congressional delegation in Washington, supported Oahe. Opposition came mainly from farmers in the path of the canals and other project features; from environmentalists wary that the James River would be channelized; and from landowners who were actually scheduled to have Oahe waters irrigate their lands.

This last group's opposition surprised many people, including congressmen, who had trouble comprehending feverish opposition from the very people who were supposedly to benefit most from the project. But the farmers feared Oahe's irrigation would salt up their already productive croplands. And they had no desire to help pay for a project they viewed as wasteful and destructive.

Opponents to Oahe formed the United Family Farmers and gained control of the local, elected board overseeing development and promotion of the project. After a series of heated public hearings, the board asked Congress to deauthorize Oahe. With only the project's pumphouse and a short length of the main canal built, Oahe was deauthorized in 1982.

Landowners and environmentalists rejoiced, but the celebration was brief. To the north, North Dakota's Garrison Project was slowly being built, and new Garrison plans called for the drainage of the project's return flows down the James River into South Dakota. The threat to the James and its bottomlands remained.

These efforts by the Bureau of Reclamation to develop irrigation projects east of the Missouri River represented a dramatic shift in thinking from those who advocated irrigation before the Pick-Sloan era. Both Garrison and Oahe proposed to irrigate productive lands with far less likelihood of drought than lands west of the 100th meridian. Early projects had been located in the drier portions of the northern plains.

Success had thus far eluded the Bureau in the northern plains. Its earliest attempts failed because the lands it chose did not respond well to irrigation and suffered alkaline buildup from poor drainage. High costs also handicapped the projects. The Bureau didn't seem to learn from its early mistakes. Farmers in Oahe's irrigation districts distrusted the Bureau's soil classifications and conducted tests that contradicted Bureau reports.

With the demise of Oahe, Garrison became the premier symbol of Pick-Sloan irrigation development in the region. But Garrison, too, was assailed by disgruntled landowners and environmentalists. The Audubon Society, disturbed by Garrison's threat to prairie wetlands and national wildlife refuges, spearheaded efforts to derail the project. Canadians grew edgy at the prospect of polluted irrigation return flows from Garrison entering the Hudson Bay watershed and harming Manitoba fisheries. They also feared the introduction of Missouri River species. Further worsening the project's reputation was the questionable cost-benefit ratio. Under steady lobbying, Congress reacted and Garrison's funding slowed to a trickle.

But in 1984, Garrison was resurrected. The Audubon Society helped formulate a commission approach to settling the Garrison debate, and the commission eventually decided on a new direction for the project. Irrigation for lands draining into Canada were dropped, settling the international dispute. To compensate, new tracts were proposed that drain into the James River. In May 1986, the commission's compromise plan became law.

To handle the increased flows, channelization of the James in North Dakota is planned. South Dakotans are unsure what to expect, but those who fought Oahe's James River channelization fear the worst.

Jay Davis, executive director of the United Family Farmers, says, "With nearly all Garrison's polluted returnflows redirected to the James River, rich farmland and wildlife habitat in South Dakota may be turned into a sterile salt marsh from fluctuating flows flooding the valley." Davis adds that the tragedy is harder to take because South Dakotans had little input into the commission plan.

North Dakota Audubon Society members say they are angry at the organization's national leadership and view the commission compromise as a sellout. One Audubon chapter, based in eastern North Dakota, sent a brochure to Audubon chapters and other conservation groups nationwide. The headline reads: "For over a decade, Audubon members throughout the nation have worked to save this river (the

James River). Today, Audubon's leadership is encouraging the river's destruction."

In an April 1986 memorandum to Audubon chapter leaders, National Audubon President Peter Berle admits the compromise is not perfect and that "some environmental damage will occur as a result of it." Berle also stresses "the compromise is a far better deal for the environment than the alternative project configuration."

That may be true in an overall sense. But Garrison threats to the James ecosystem, serious under the original Garrison plan and made more serious by the commission plan, could one day claim the river as a sacrifice for water development. The irony of the threat to the James River and its valley is that Garrison promoters cite the loss of the natural Missouri River and its many thousands of acres of bottomlands as the reason North Dakota is owed Garrison.

In November 1980, South Dakota Governor William Janklow proposed that the Garrison Diversion Unit be extended into his state. As the idea was studied and expanded, it became known as Garrison Extension. Water provided by Garrison would be utilized for irrigation, industrial and municipal uses. Attracting the same type of support as the Oahe Project, Garrison Extension focuses unprecedented attention on the James River in South Dakota. Plans to alter the channel to increase its water-carrying capacity gained support in the state's water development community and forged a revived enthusiasm for Garrison as the feeder supply for Garrison Extension. With the South Dakota Department of Water and Natural Resources coordinating efforts to promote Garrison Extension, river modification was soon underway.

In northern South Dakota, on one of the James' most scenic stretches, a dredging operation is deepening and trenching the river. Prohibitive costs and mismanagement may halt the dredging, but appropriations in the water omnibus bill now under consideration by Congress could continue river alteration.

In a land of few rivers, with the vast, open countryside filled with agricultural enterprise, the James and its valley are a narrow corridor where nature survives. One hundred and fifty miles of the river in northern South Dakota is eligible for inclusion in the nation's wild and scenic rivers program. Three federal wildlife refuges straddle the river, attesting to the river system's role in the central flyway for migrating birds. Along the length of the river riparian woodlands and wetlands provide irreplaceable habitat for wild creatures and a haven for those who enjoy the outdoors.

The James is a river of significance, the longest tributary of the Missouri River, but it is also a river long targeted by water developers

Workers build the Belle Fourche Dam, South Dakota, 1910

hoping to use it as a conduit for return flows or as a water delivery or water storage system for irrigation and industrial growth. The river's values as a natural system are largely unappreciated, and the attitude threatening the James is no different from the attitude that destroyed the Missouri.

The northern plains is a region where, because so much depends on agricultural productivity, preservation of the landscape, rivers, and wetlands has not come first. Current agricultural practices and the importance of stabilizing the region's farm-based economy puts relentless pressure on resources.

And that brings us back to Campbell and his dry-land approach to farming, versus rainmaking and irrigation. Should the region's agriculture conform to the environment of the region, or should the environment of the region be transformed?

In part, the answer will depend on economics. But it will also depend on people learning to appreciate the beauty and character of a difficult region. It is still too early to tell, but it appears that residents are slowly awakening to the importance of safeguarding the natural resources that remain in their heavily agricultural states. The environmental consciousness that began on the east and west coasts has found its way to the nation's most remote hinterland. Today, it is difficult to fathom a river perishing without a tussle as did the Missouri.

17

How Could Anyone Oppose, or Favor, the Garrison Project?

Ed Marston

How could anyone oppose the Garrison Diversion Project?

North Dakota saw several hundred thousand acres of fertile Missouri River bottomland buried beneath the Army Corps' Pick-Sloan reservoirs for the benefit of downstream states. North Dakota is a young state — its centennial is still several years away — and it needs help from older states. Along with its youth, North Dakota is rural — 25 percent of its 670,000 people live on farms. These farmers are asking the rest of America to help them be more stable and productive. Long droughts, such as hit in the 1930s, eroded land, wiped out mother herds of cows and pigs, and drove 10 percent of the people off their farms and out of the state. After the droughts, agriculture had to start over, renewing the land and rebuilding the herds. A large irrigation project could anchor the state.

How could anyone be for Garrison?

Depending on the version of the project, Garrison would indeed put from 130,000 to one million acres into irrigation. But the mid-sized 250,000-acre version would simultaneously remove 230,000

Lyle Axthelme, BuRec

Garrison Dam, North Dakota

acres from cultivation for canal right-of-way and wildlife mitigation. The newly irrigated land would produce crops already in surplus. The 250,000-acre project would create 1300 farms at a cost to taxpayers of about $4000 for each irrigated acre, or $700,000 a farm. It would devastate 12 wildlife refuges, eliminate 180,000 ducks a year and 70,000 acres of waterfowl marsh, and send water polluted with pesticides and foreign organisms from the Missouri River basin into Canada's Hudson Bay. Canadians fear that would devastate their fisheries. Even with all the damage, Garrison would irrigate less than one percent of North Dakota's farmland and have a vanishingly small effect on the economy.

T hose contradictory questions cannot be answered by economic or ecological reasoning. Resolution depends on seeing Garrison as symbol and history rather than concrete. It is a project that caught the imagination of America's coldest, most isolated state at birth, and it is a symbol that North Dakota is only now reluctantly releasing.

The letting go has taken the form of a compromise. The irrigation acreage for Garrison has been scaled back from the original one million acres in the project authorized by Congress in 1965 ("A sacred promise," project promoters call it) to 130,000 acres. And 17,000 acres of that will go to the three Fort Berthold Reservation tribes that were criminally abused by the Army Corps of Engineers in the construction of Garrison Dam. (See map on pages 108–109.) The original proposal had no Indian lands in it.

None of the irrigated acreage will be in the Hudson Bay drainage, and the 12 wildlife preserves have been spared. Thus far, 85,000 acres have been identified for irrigation, including 36,000 acres now wetlands or other wildlife habitat. The Bureau of Reclamation says that lost habitat will be more than replaced — the Bureau will provide 63,000 acres of wetlands, woodlands, and pasture. The wetlands will be created by buying drained farmland, and then filling in the drainage ditches or turning off the pumps that keep the land dry and farmable.

Garrison, as approved by Congress in May 1986, will cost $1.2 billion. Originally, Garrison was all irrigation. But even North Dakota must shift away from total dependence on farming, so $200 million will be spent to provide drinking water to North Dakota's towns and cities. The law also created a Wetlands Trust to save wetlands from draining and farming.

The 1986 law also appears to save the Lonetree Reservoir site. That site was craved by promoters of the big project because it could take water from the Missouri and distribute it to three river basins. One of those, the James River basin, is within the Missouri basin; the other two are to the northwest in the Hudson Bay drainage. The Bureau, once on the verge of building Lonetree, ends up owning a 33,000-acre site. The site will stay in wildlife, but the 1986 law says it may someday become a reservoir for an expanded project if it can satisfy Canadian and other concerns. The new law does spare fecund Kraft Slough near the South Dakota border, which was to be the site of the 2,680-acre Taayer Reservoir.

On the other side of the ecological scale is a heavyweight — the James River. It is America's longest non-navigable river — a muddy, slow-moving body of water that is also fertile fish, bird, and wildlife habitat. The compromise has set the James River up for destruction. Pending two years of experiments with 5000 acres of irrigated ground and studies of the river, it may be channelized to carry the water that will flow off 130,000 acres of newly irrigated land. Channelization would physically destroy much wildlife habitat; the flow of irrigation drainage could poison surviving wildlife, as has happened at places such as Kesterson Wildlife Refuge in California.

Politically, the compromise frees the National Audubon Society from what it has apparently come to see as an albatross. Environmental groups are creatures of the philanthropic and public interest marketplace. The organization fought Garrison with all its resources until three years ago; then, under new leadership, it decided its time and money could be better spent elsewhere.

North Dakota's national politicians (two senators and one congressman), by biting the Garrison bullet, will also be able to go on to other issues, if they survive the next few elections. The first test came in November 1986 soon after Congress approved the Garrison compromise. Republican incumbent Senator Mark Andrews lost to Democratic challenger Kent Conrad. The major issue was the dismal farm economy. Whatever glory may have accrued to Andrews as a result of the Garrison compromise wasn't enough to save him.

Some say the destruction of the James River accompanies the destruction of a North Dakota dream: that the treeless, flat, dry Missouri River basin part of the state could be made more eastern, more humid, more stable. Garrison, at its most extravagant, could confer that benefit on only a small part of the state and a few of its farmers. But that did not seem to matter, no more than it matters that the nation can send only a handful of people to the moon.

Garrison was symbolic in another way. North Dakota is not only a new state — it is a foreign state, settled by people who came directly from farming villages in northern Europe to farming villages in North Dakota. Some third generation North Dakotans will speak with traces of accents. Unlike neighboring Wyoming, with its transplanted New England heritage and sense of ease in New York or Washington, North Dakota was cut off from the Eastern power centers by distance and culture.

The touchiness of North Dakota — its quickness to embrace conspiracy theories and radical political parties, the ease with which it moves from boosting to blaming — may come from a painful awareness of its welfare status. The state is dependent not only on farm programs, but also on defense, highways, and the like. North Dakota is no different in this from other Western states, but lacks the psychological trick of burying that federal dependency under the image of a lean, independent man on horseback.

Garrison was going to eliminate its dependency with one last burst of federal generosity: a few billion dollars to help create a strong, drought-resistant agricultural economy.

That vision is vanishing, along with many small towns in arid western North Dakota — towns populated by elderly people who have memories but no dreams. The wheat farmers in that region's droughty climate and marginal soils were kept in business by federal farm programs. Now the subsidy programs are being withdrawn. They have been replaced by a land withdrawal, or conservation, program that pays farmers to put wheatfields into grass.

None of the above explains or justifies even a scaled-down Garrison; not when farmers in southern California's fertile valleys can't make their irrigated land pay. But the United States doesn't run by economic logic alone. The people of North Dakota have a huge political investment in Garrison. Their senators and congressmen for a century maneuvered onto committees that could move Garrison. In pursuit of Garrison, the state ignored or traded away other opportunities.

In the American system, something is owed the state for all those years. If a state has a collective personality, North Dakota's has a chip on its shoulder. The state fears it may not be as good as the rest of America, and it is ready to fight to prove itself wrong.

So the Gramm-Rudman-Hollings Congress, from exasperation, from log rolling, and perhaps from environmentalist miscalculation, has decided it is best to give way. The genius of American politics is to avoid fights to the death. It is expedient and pragmatic rather than principled and ideological.

No one will write a ballad about the Saga of Garrison, or even an heroic couplet. But this compromise, with its destruction of the James River, may allow everyone, especially North Dakotans, the freedom to think about what North Dakota is good for.

18

The Real Water Lawyers

Marjane Ambler

For nearly a decade, lawyers for the state of Wyoming have battled attorneys representing the Wind River Reservation for the waters of the Wind River - Big Horn River.

The state filed the lawsuit in 1977 as a pre-emptive strike against a possible Indian suit based on their Winters Doctrine water rights. If the state, which moved into the suit with secrecy and speed, had hoped for a quick victory over unprepared Indians, they miscalculated. The suit is now an institution involving 25,000 Wyoming water users, documents measured by the roomsfull, $10 million in expenses to the state and millions to the Indians and federal government.

A decision by water-court referee and former Democratic Congressman Teno Roncalio and a subsequent Wyoming court has awarded the Indians a large amount of water and a very early priority date. The result has been near panic among non-Indian irrigators who share water with the Shoshone and Arapahoe tribes.

As of spring 1987, the case had been argued before the Wyoming Supreme Court, but no decision had been handed down. Unless there is a negotiated settlement, it will almost certainly reach the United States Supreme Court.

Sara Hunter-Wiles

William Wagon and irrigation measuring device on the Wind River Reservation

But here on the Wind River Reservation, where Indian and non-Indian farmers share the water in the Wind River Irrigation Project, no one can wait for the lawyers to turn the water onto the fields of its legal owners. Even if the lawyers were so inclined, it is doubtful they could get the water onto the right fields in the right amount. The physical operation of an irrigation system is as complex as the adjudication of water rights.

The physical "adjudication" of water from the Wind River Irrigation Project is done by seven ditch riders and two supervisors, the water masters. All are employed by the Bureau of Indian Affairs, which is responsible for the project.

Each day they decide who gets how much water. The ditch riders use "turn-on cards," which are primitive water-measuring devices, arithmetic, and above all, diplomacy. The nine are all Indians, and although 70 percent of the project land is owned by the tribes or by individual Indians, 70 percent of the land is farmed by non-Indians.

Pending resolution of the lawsuit, the ditch riders base their on-the-ground allocation on demand and on what amounts of water they know can be put to use. Crops in this dry climate need to have five acre-feet spread over them during a summer. Three of those acre-feet

The low-tech art of irrigating

The Upper Missouri River basin lands of the western Dakotas and eastern Montana and Wyoming get enough rain for livestock grazing. But, as in much of the arid West, irrigation is often required to grow crops. Irrigation projects have made the region a mix of large stretches of dry country interrupted here and there by "patches" of green made all the more vivid by the surrounding brown land.

Some of the green patches are small, isolated fields in flat places where it was possible to divert water directly out of rivers or streams. Other "patches," thousands to tens of thousands of acres in extent, are "projects": large storage dams on rivers, wide canals to deliver water from the dams to the project, and hundreds of miles of small, branching canals or pipes to give each acre access to water. How much water? Typically, an acre of irrigated crop requires three to five acre-feet of water each summer. (An acre-foot covers an acre of land to a depth of one foot.)

In theory, an irrigation system is simple. In practice, it is complex. The ditches are usually dirt, and may seep. They are 19th century technology in the late 20th century. Many canals were built in the late 19th or early 20th century, and are a part of the West's infrastructure that is most worn out.

The projects almost always depend on gravity to lead the water to the land. As a result, the main canals must follow gently sloping contours. This usually means the canals are both long and unstable, since they must hug miles of hillsides liable to slumping and sliding. The nightmare of every Western irrigator is a slide

that wipes out a critical canal in the middle of August.

There are also problems once the water reaches the project. Water measurement is often rough. On many systems, it is measured by the height of the water as it flows through a narrowed section of canal, or by how many times a valve handle is turned in a large pipe leading to a section of fields, or by the width of an opening created by a board that slices water out of the main canal and puts it in a lateral ditch.

A single lateral ditch may serve several farmers, and if too many of the farmers want to irrigate at once, the ones at the end may be dry. So ditch riders must forever be roaming the area, shutting off some farmers and sending water to others. Irrigation in the West is labor-intensive, and thus expensive.

Another complication is the way fields sit one above the other. If the fields are watered by sprinkler systems, that vertical distribution of land doesn't matter because little water will run off. But most Western irrigators simply dump water onto their fields, letting it run along furrows, or marks, from the high to the low end. About half the water is taken up by plants or evaporates. The other half sinks into the ground to appear downhill as seep or spring water, or flows off the field on the surface.

A careful farmer will collect his surface waste water in a ditch running along the low end of his field and deliver it, in one place, to the downhill neighbor. But a farmer who is sloppy or who wishes to bedevil his neighbor, can cause no end of misery by letting water run off uncontrolled. In such cases, crops can be washed

Lyle Axthelm, BuRec

Water in the Helena Valley, Montana, flows from the delivery canal in the foreground through the gates to the small canal serving the field. Water is supplied to the moveable sprinkler by pumps.

out of the ground and fields eroded in a short time.

In the early years of the West's settlement, a family or group of families could, with shovels and horsedrawn scrapers, build an irrigation system. They could put in a headgate on a stream, and use it to divert the stream into a canal for distribution to nearby flat fields. These direct-flow systems were fine so long as the creek ran all summer. Many creeks, however, slow to a trickle in August. Then farmers even in these favored streamside locations were limited to one cutting of alfalfa in the early summer, followed by prayers for a late rain.

So, throughout the West, large federally built and subsidized irrigation projects became the order of the day. With the help of federal engineering expertise, federal capital, and often federal arm-twisting to force the area's farmers to pool their water rights, large reservoirs were built to catch spring runoff and hold it until river flows dropped. The projects included lengthy systems of canals to get the water to flat, fertile lands far from the river and main reservoir itself.

Many parts of the West have two kinds of such projects: one built by the Bureau of Reclamation for white settlers (often on former Indian land), and one built by the Bureau of Indian Affairs for its Indian clients.

Two examples of those projects sit literally facing each other along the Wind River/Big Horn River in central Wyoming, the BuRec's Midvale District and the BIA's Wind River Irrigation District. In addition to their physical proximity, their fates have been intertwined in the past and, after following parallel paths for decades, have again come together in the 1980s.

—*Ed Marston*

will seep into or flow over the ground and reappear elsewhere. Two acre-feet will evaporate or be taken up by the crops.

The system is rough. Ditch riders lack devices to accurately allocate the water and must make decisions based on experience and common sense. The inaccuracy is not confined to reservations; sloppy allocation of irrigation water is typical in the West, where each acre of alfalfa or corn yearly consumes enough water to support 10 urban residents.

Were the water precisely measured out, the ditch rider's job would be simpler. But because he must make subjective judgments, he gets heat from farmers who think they've been shorted.

"Some people think I just get in my pickup and ride around all day. It looks easy but it's not," says William Wagon, a Shoshone Indian and a ditch rider for 16 years before he became a water master. With 400 miles of ditches, the water masters and ditch riders do a lot of riding. Each ditch rider is responsible for daily checking of headgates that serve about 5000 acres of land. Wagon figures he covers 100 miles a day, mostly over dirt lanes that parallel the ditches. He can't count how many times he gets out to open a wire gate in a day. Cattleguards, like precise water measuring devices, would make the ditch riders and farmers more productive, but the project can't afford them.

Wagon's year starts in the spring, when the water is turned into the ditch after the winter. His day then begins at 6 a.m. with the checking of the card boxes where farmers leave their daily requests for water, and the gauges. Then he clears rubble deposited by winter and spring runoff out of the lateral ditches — ditches that run off the main canal to the farmers.

Early in the season, when the main canal and laterals are still seepy from the winter dryout and the various gates may not be working well, Wagon may work until 9 p.m. to make sure everyone is getting water. Then he may get called out at midnight by a farmer who is getting no water, or who is getting flooded.

In an ideal world, each farmer would get the water he wanted when he wanted it. But a single lateral serving 20 farmers may be only large enough to provide 10 of them with water at any one time. So when Wagon reads the cards left by the irrigators, and finds that 15 farmers want water on a lateral built for 10, he makes a decision that is going to irritate five people. If someone complains about the consequences of this daily juggling act, which includes making sure some water is left in the river for fish, Wagon tells him: "You have to do with what you got."

Wagon says it is the mental pressure from conflicting demands that usually gets to new ditch riders. "You have people jumping on you. Some farmers take what they get — others don't."

Wagon's sense of humor and good nature probably account for his ability to withstand the stress. Swinging up the trail to check the Ray Canal gauge, he walks with the wide gait of a man who spends much of his time in irrigation boots. He says that farmers who fight all summer become friends again in the winter. "We're all like big children. That's what I've noticed."

Summer 1985 was particularly difficult because grasshoppers and a drought coincided. The acting project manager, Louis Twitchell, decided to rotate the irrigators — 10 days with water and 10 days without. The water masters and ditch riders had to enforce the decision.

Allison Sage, an Arapahoe ditch rider, says a couple of disputes erupted into fist fights. But he and his cohorts were usually able to explain the rotation and head off other disputes.

Sage and Wagon know first hand that in the West, fighting over water can be done in various ways. One farmer may flood a downhill neighbor's field on purpose, washing out his crop. Or he can pull a checkboard at night to increase the flow to his own field and decrease the flow to his neighbor's field. Or he may put rocks or sod in the ditch to divert water to his field and away from his neighbor's.

As a result of the games people play, Wagon says the favorite part of his job is winter. "I don't have to fight with nobody. I just keep busy, trying to get repairs done."

William Wagon   Allison Sage

Ditch rider Sage, 51, sees his job as a base from which to improve the reservation. He's a teacher, but the ditch riding allows him to live on his home reservation and be with his family on weekends. It also lets him serve on the school board, of which he's chairman.

A big man, husky and over six feet tall, Sage wants the children in his schools to one day develop a reservation economy, with agriculture a major part of the base. As a first step to that end, three years ago the Arapahoe people took over the local school from the Bureau of Indian Affairs (BIA), and knocked the dropout rate way down, Sage says.

The potential for change is great. Non-Indians farm most of the land, and 8000 acres within the irrigation project lie idle. Those lands don't produce crops or pay operation and maintenance fees to help support an aged, deteriorating project.

Sage hopes to see the idle land put back into production under the plows of Indian landowners. But there are obstacles. "A lot of kids don't know how to drive tractors or irrigate." Many of their parents are BIA boarding-school products and weren't taught such skills.

By the time the young people now in the reservation's schools are old enough to farm, the farmer's and ditch rider's world will be different. The settlement of the lawsuit will certainly require that today's eyeball approach to water allocation be replaced by a precise system. But for now, Twitchell and the men under him concentrate on getting water to the alfalfa and barley fields while cooling down farmers who need cooling down.

19

A Tale of Two Irrigation Districts

Marjane Ambler

S hoshone and Arapahoe ditch riders who patrol the Bureau of Indian Affairs' Wind River Irrigation Project sometimes look longingly across the river. The modern, efficient Midvale project reminds them of the unrealized potential of their own project.

Midvale looks especially good because the U.S. Bureau of Reclamation recently put $46 million into upgrading Midvale. But the Arapahoe-Shoshone project has not received federal construction money since 1979, and in 1985 federal help for operating costs was withdrawn, too.

"Just look across the river, and you can see the tremendous job they're doing. We're just holding the line here," says Louis Twitchell, a Shoshone and acting manager of the Wind River Project. While his tribe and the Midvale irrigators have been battling in the courts for years, he leaves the fighting to the attorneys and politicians and expresses only envy when asked about Midvale.

Across the river, Midvale Manager Jack Long avoids any criticism of the Indian project. He attributes Midvale's better shape partly to its aggressiveness in raising the farmer's operation and maintenance fees. Midvale, which has 60,000 acres, charges water users $560 for 40 acres, compared to the $436 the BIA water users pay.

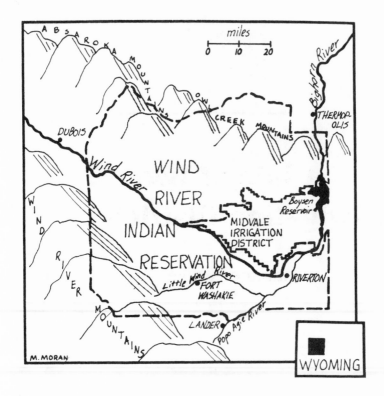

But without the recent federally funded improvements, Long says his project would be in trouble. The Bureau of Reclamation lined canals and laterals, installed pipes to replace some ditches, buried 300 miles of pipe drains to draw water off saturated lands, and modified a diversion dam. Long says, "It would be inoperable now without the improvements."

Long and other state political leaders convinced Congress in 1970 to spend $12.1 million on Midvale. When the work was completed in 1986 it had cost $45.6 million. Some of that money will be repaid by Midvale's water users at a rate of 50 cents to $2.05 an acre for 50 years. Most of it will come out of hydroelectric revenues from urban users.

The Shoshone-Arapahoe irrigation project didn't get a federally financed upgrade, and it is not clear that the aging project will be able to keep operating as concrete drops and chutes deteriorate, ditch banks erode, steel gates rust, and wood timbers rot. Twitchell says, "We try to keep it patched up, but reason dictates that it will catch up with us eventually."

As a result, the project's land-base is dropping. More than 10,000 acres can't be assessed operation fees because they are no longer usable. Twitchell says thousands of acres have become saturated because of inadequate drainage on lands above them. They could be reclaimed, he says, but there is no money to install drains.

In addition to the waterlogged land, 8000 farmable acres of the 40,000-acre project lie idle. Most are idle because, through inheritance, small tracts of land have been split among 200 or 300 people, and leasing it to one farmer is impractical. The problem also complicates the collection of operations and maintenance fees.

The operations and maintenance budget is further eroded because the Shoshone and Arapahoe tribes refuse to pay fees for tribally owned lands. That cut 11 percent, or $40,000, from the project's hard-pressed budget in 1985. The dispute is said to be close to resolution, but even an extra $40,000 a year won't solve the project's problems.

The existing farmers are unlikely to accept further fee hikes. When Idaho Republican Senator James McClure's appropriations committee eliminated operating subsidies for all Category I Indian projects in 1984, farmers' fees increased 70 percent in two years, from $6.40 to $10.90 an acre. The jumps came amidst a terrible farm economy.

Bob Delk disagrees with the congressional decision to cut off supplemental aid to the project. The chief of BIA water services out of Billings, Montana, Delk says Indian projects in the Billings area cannot support themselves since none have been completed.

Technically, they have been completed. The BIA "completed" them by designating Wind River and four of the five BIA projects in Montana as Category I, or complete, projects. But Delk says, "We never reached the design level on any of them." Larger projects cost less to operate on a per-acre basis than incomplete projects, which means lower per-acre fees. The Catch 22 is that Wind River (and the other Indian projects) can't be completed because Congress has not supplied construction money since 1979.

Phil Corke has been fighting for Indian irrigation funding for close to 20 years within the BIA in Washington, D.C. He was hopeful in the late 1970s, for despite Jimmy Carter's opposition to most federal water projects, the president favored funding Indian projects. Corke says that momentum was lost when the administration changed.

Now Corke fights the attitude — both within the BIA and the Office of Management and Budget — that putting money into irrigation projects is like "pouring money down a rathole." He says people think Indians get unfair advantages because they don't repay construction costs. Since non-Indians repay only about 10 percent of the costs of their projects, Corke finds little difference between Indian and non-Indian projects.

The problems facing Indian irrigation districts are rooted in history. With the creation at the turn of the century of the Reclamation Service, now the U.S. Bureau of Reclamation, and its placement in the Department of Interior with the Bureau of Indian Affairs, conflicts erupted. The government opened many riverside reservations to homesteading, including several in the upper Missouri basin.

Indians and Indian advocates began a continuing battle for rights to water and money for irrigation projects. They also had to hold onto their irrigable land, and keep it from being sold or leased, or inundated under BuRec reservoirs built to supply non-Indian irrigation projects with water.

Often they lost those battles. Most of the Missouri basin's major Army Corps of Engineers and BuRec dams — Boysen, Yellowtail, Fort Peck, Garrison, Oahe, Big Bend, Fort Randall and Gavins Point — inundated Indian lands or backed water up over the Indian lands.

On the other hand, Indian irrigation projects benefited from the reservation land sales; money for several major Indian projects — including Wind River — came directly from such sales.

In 1905, the Shoshone and Arapahoe tribes, under federal pressure, ceded 1.5 million acres of reservation land north of the Big Wind River to the government for homesteading.

Some of the remaining Indian land was already irrigated. Shoshone tribal members had started digging their own ditches in 1882. Historian Peter Iverson says the Indians' early success could be measured by an 1898 report that they supplied their own needs as well as sending 800,000 pounds of hay, 760,000 pounds of oats, and 585,000 pounds of wheat to the federal Indian agency, Fort Washakie, and the school.

With the money from the 1.5 million acre land sale and tribal members' hard work, Wind River became one of the better-developed reservations in the nation. Later, when the Indians were asked to pay $1 an acre water charge, they objected vehemently. Tribal delegates went to Washington, D.C., to argue that the 1905 cession agreement provided for government financing of the project and that they had dug the ditches themselves. Moreover, by the 1920s, many tribal members could not afford food, much less the water charge, according to historian Loretta Fowler. When they could not pay the fees, the BIA encouraged them to lease or sell their land, further eroding the Indian land base.

In 1934, federal Indian policies reversed again, and the Roosevelt administration returned thousands of ceded acres that had not been homesteaded to Indian ownership, including 981,000 acres of the Wind River Reservation north of the river.

Midvale, however, was not returned, and settlers continued to claim land there as late as 1950, according to newspaper reports. Now

Midvale is prosperous and efficient, but it is on land that was originally Indian and it is opposite a decaying Indian project.

Ironically, Midvale may now benefit the Arapahoe and Shoshone tribal members. Basically, the tribes hope to trade their smashing courtroom water-rights victory for development money.

Wyoming has been forced to the bargaining table to protect Midvale and other non-Indians from losing water to the Indians during water-short years. As mentioned earlier, the Wyoming District Court in 1984 awarded the Shoshone and Arapahoe tribes much more water than Wyoming anticipated when the state filed its 1977 lawsuit.

Although some aspects may be changed by the Wyoming Supreme Court on appeal, the state estimates that the tribes could cut off water to between 11,000 and 50,000 acres now irrigated by non-Indians.

"They could wipe out the Midvale Irrigation District," says R.T. Cox, one of the attorneys representing Wyoming in the litigation.

Based upon a 1908 U.S. Supreme Court decision known as the Winters Doctrine, tribes have rights to the water necessary to make their reservations into permanent homelands. The priority date is based on when the reservation was established. The Wyoming District Court ruled that the Shoshone and Arapahoe tribes could divert 477,000 acre-feet, the amount it determined necessary for irrigation. With this, the tribes could put about 60,000 new acres under irrigation. With a priority date of 1868, the Indian rights predate everyone else.

However, the paper rights won't help the tribes without more storage and irrigation development. Therefore, the tribes are also interested in negotiating a settlement to determine how water will be developed and used.

Under the preliminary terms of the proposed settlement, Wyoming would provide about $45 million in state funds as well as its clout in seeking another $50 million from the federal government. The tribes would agree to defer using some of their water. By also providing for new storage and tribal rights to existing Boysen Reservoir storage, the agreement would protect the rights of non-Indians at Midvale and elsewhere in the Big Horn River drainage.

Funding for rehabilitating the existing Bureau of Indian Affairs Wind River Irrigation Project has been considered but is not an integral part of the negotiations at this time, according to Tom Fredericks, an attorney who represents the Arapahoe Tribe.

Fredericks, who once served as assistant secretary for Indian affairs in Washington, D.C., believes the BIA should be providing money for upkeep of existing irrigation projects. He says the BIA is more concerned with social welfare than natural resources.

Tribes elsewhere in the West have met varying success in using water rights to bargain for water development. In Arizona, the tribes of the Ak-Chin and Papago reservations won water-development assistance under the Central Arizona Project after lengthy battles.

More recently, in the Missouri basin, the state of Montana reached a settlement in 1985 with the tribes of the Fort Peck Reservation that did not include money for water development. That historic agreement was the first reached by the Montana Reserved Water Rights Compact Commission, a board established by the Legislature to resolve Indian and federal water claims outside of the courts.

Fort Peck tribal leaders now hope to convince Congress to appropriate water development money as an incentive to other tribes to negotiate. The Northern Cheyenne Tribe, which has no BIA irrigation project on its lands, is seeking development funds as part of its compact with Montana.

Several water experts speculate, however, that Interior Secretary Donald Hodel enthusiastically endorses the Fort Peck Compact because the department hopes it will serve as a model for settlements without development dollars.

Part Four

The
Colorado
River
As
Plumbing

THE COLORADO RIVER BASIN

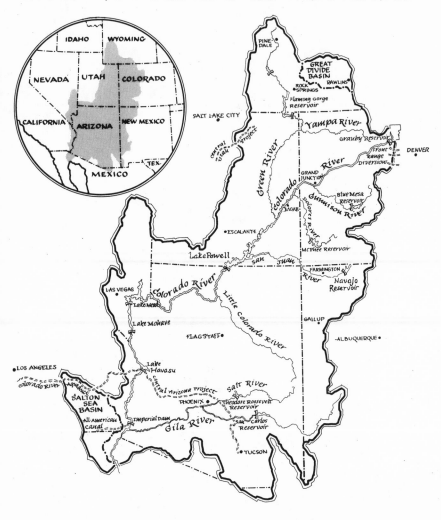

A KEY TO THE PLUMBING SYSTEM

RESERVOIRS

Less than 1.5 million   2-5 million   33-36 million

Storage Capacities, in acre-feet

WATER DIVERSIONS

0-0.6 million   1.2-2.4 million   3-35 million

Depletions, in acre-feet
(Projected figures for CAP and CUP, now under construction)

TRIBUTARY STREAMS

...AND ITS PLUMBING

MAP AND PLUMBING COMPILED
AND EDITED BY MARY MORAN
RENDERED BY LESTER DORÉ

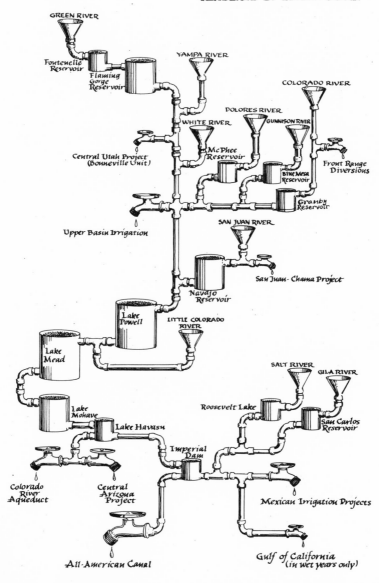

COLORADO RIVER BASIN

River Length (miles)	Basin Size (square miles)	Average Annual Runoff (acre-feet)	Average Flow at River Mouth (acre-feet)
1,450	235,000	15 million	0

Irrigated Land (acres)	Reservoir Storage — Active Capacity (acre-feet)	Hydropower Capacity (megawatts)
2.2 million	58.9 million	3,786

20

They Built Better than They Knew

Ed Marston

Philip Fradkin called the Colorado *A River No More*. Part Four of this book is titled "The Colorado River As Plumbing." The point is the same. For this geologic instant, before siltation and mudslides and tectonic twitches again take charge — man is in control of the Colorado River. His plumbing is in place, embedded beneath the Continental Divide, anchored to the walls of high canyons, dug through the shaley soil of countless hillsides.

There are lessons to be gained from arguing the morality and aesthetics of this plumbing: the loss of Glen Canyon, the gaining of hydroelectricity, the transformation of land from desert to neat rows of vegetables, the conversion of the once relatively pure lower Colorado River into a sink for salt and heavy metals in such concentrations that it stunts crops and deforms ducks.

But the American West isn't big on backward looks and moral analysis. The radical environmental group Earth First! may fantasize about the destruction of Glen Canyon Dam, but the West's environmental movement is more interested in gaining a say in the control of the plumbing than in decrying its existence.

So "a river no more" and "the river as plumbing" are deceptive phrases. The Colorado is no longer natural, but neither is it a dead-

Mel Davis, BuRec

Glen Canyon Dam and Lake Powell on the Colorado River, Utah-Arizona

and-gone river. It has been plumbed – the big projects are in place or being put in place. The billions of dollars for the huge pipes, dams, pumps, and canals have been sunk on the basis of decisions by a tiny group of men in Congress, in the Bureau of Reclamation, and in the state engineers' offices.

But the billions spent on this plumbing will now be dwarfed by tens of billions to be spent to modify it, to mitigate its impacts, and to buy out old water users and put the plumbing to new uses. The era of massive construction is about over; the much more expensive era of nudging the river into a modified shape is just beginning.

As Part One showed, at the national level, the plumbers – the Bureau of Reclamation and the Corps of Engineers – are dying or renewing themselves, attempting to escape old roles and adapt to new. Chapter 5, in its look at Sulphur Springs Valley, Arizona, and California's Imperial Irrigation District, also showed old economic uses – the growing of hay, cotton and other commodity crops – being driven out, with the pressure on to convert the water to other uses.

The Columbia and Missouri help to explain the Colorado. They drain interesting regions, but compared with the Colorado River, they are one-note rivers: In the Dakotas, the Missouri, deserted by the era that spawned the Pick-Sloan plan, has no visible alternatives for change. It seems stuck with enormous reservoirs that produce some hydroelectricity and float a few barges in the lower basin. In the Northwest, the Columbia is dominated by the competition between hydropower and salmon. The river was developed mainly for hydropower in a sledgehammer approach dictated by a single federal agency — the Bonneville Power Administration.

The Colorado has developed in a more diverse way. The 1922 Colorado River Compact reserved for each of the seven basin states some portion of the river's annual flow of 14 to 18 million acre-feet (the range depends on which series of years you average). Without that appointment, southern California's farms and cities would have drunk the river dry in the years after World War II. The region would also have consumed all of the Colorado's hydropower to light its cities and power the pumps that lift Colorado River water over the mountains to the coastal plain.

Saving the Colorado River from California also required a federal policy directed at helping all seven states develop their compact-share of the Colorado. The main federal instrument of this policy was the U.S. Bureau of Reclamation. That agency robbed Indian tribes of land and water; it proceeded with reckless disregard of the environment; it at times made stunning engineering errors.

That was the fallout, the side effects, of a populist policy intended to put tens of thousands of people on the land and to economically anchor hundreds of small communities in the rural West. At its most idealistic, the Bureau was a mechanism for spending hundreds of millions of dollars to create independent farmers and ranchers in the upper basin states of Colorado, Utah, Wyoming and New Mexico. It is no accident that part of the Bureau's funding came from federal mineral-lease income. The Bureau's projects were ways for the West to convert its mined minerals into more permanent wealth.

In southern California, Bureau projects often went to agribusiness. But in the upper basin, many small projects on the main-stem Colorado and its tributaries still keep, even in these difficult times, rural communities from blowing away. Grand Junction, Colorado, near the Utah border, is most famous for its 1982 oil shale bust. The town is in bad shape; it would be in worse shape if not for 70,000 acres of fertile land in the Grand Valley irrigated by a mix of private and federal projects.

The Grand Valley is the last major irrigation project on the upper Colorado River. It is one of the last places on the upper Colorado where major water diversions are possible without pumping. Beyond the Grand Valley, the Colorado separates from the land, sinking into the canyon country of Utah and then into the Grand Canyon of Arizona.

Below the Grand Canyon, only big straws are put into the river: the Central Arizona Project, southern California's Colorado River Aqueduct, the Imperial and Coachello valleys' diversions.

There is some flexibility in the lower basin, but it is the flexibility of elephants. Southern California cities are looking at Imperial's excess water; the Central Arizona Project's water will first be used for crops, but then, as Phoenix-Tucson grows, it will be converted to municipal and industrial use. Agriculture is slated to die. Even in the productive Arizona and California valleys, irrigated agriculture is seen as stopgap: a 100-year-long activity that will be bought out or forced out by urbanization.

Part Four is not about the lower Colorado River basin. The only lower basin chapter concerns Mexico's Mexicali Valley. It shows how the 1900s' effort to harness the Colorado River in its lowest reaches sent waves upriver. Efforts to divert the Colorado into the Imperial Valley and to Los Angeles forced the creation of the 1922 Colorado River Compact and construction of Hoover Dam. Today, by forcing major salinity projects on it, those lower reaches of the Colorado are still shaping the upper basin.

No one knows what is a trend, what is a spike, what is a misinterpretation of data. With that disclaimer, it appears that the trend in the upper basin is toward a rapid decline of agriculture and a slower decline in the value of hydroelectricity relative to other water uses.

There are many examples. For decades, the Shoshone hydroelectric power plant in Colorado's Glenwood Canyon dominated the paper Colorado River. The "paper" river is that collection of water rights and laws that determines where the plumbing will direct the wet river to flow. Shoshone's hydroelectric right required that upstream diverters such as Denver, which takes water out of the high mountains for diversion eastward under the Continental Divide, permit at least 1250 cubic feet per second to stay in the river for use by Shoshone. That water is then run through Shoshone's turbines to make electricity.

But in 1986, Denver and Public Service Company, which owns Shoshone and its water rights, struck a deal. Denver can reduce the river's flow below 1250 cfs so long as it reimburses PSCo for the lost electricity. The foregone electricity is worth a pittance compared to the value of the water to Front Range cities.

If the courts agree, that deal will drastically alter the paper river. Hundreds of water rights downstream of Shoshone on the Colorado were sheltered in that 1250 cfs flow. The holders of those rights, some of which are used now and some of which are planned for development, face a new world.

Stuart T. Wagner

The Shoshone hydroelectric power plant, Colorado

More important than the direct effect of the deal is its precedent. Upper Colorado River reservoirs such as the 1.2 million acre-foot Blue Mesa on the Gunnison River in western Colorado and the 4.7 million acre-foot Flaming Gorge on Utah and Wyoming's Green River have little function apart from hydroelectricity.

In Colorado, those hydroelectric rights set limits on the amount of water Denver, Aurora, Colorado Springs or whoever can take from the upper reaches of the Gunnison or Colorado for diversion to the Front Range. But Shoshone demonstrates that the paper river can be altered. Low-value hydropower can be suborned to high-value urban development. The fact that the U.S. Bureau of Reclamation will make the decision at most hydropower dams rather than an electric company does not change matters over the long run.

Right now, the plumbing in the upper Colorado River is managed mainly for hydroelectricity. Neither Colorado nor Wyoming come close to using their compact allotments of Colorado River water. The economic, demographic truth is that there are not enough farmers, industry, and towns and cities in the upper basin to soak up the water impounded in its reservoirs. To the east, the Denver Front Range farmers and cities divert some water into the Missouri River basin for their use. But Colorado-Wyoming-Utah still send several million acre-feet downstream each year for California, and now Arizona, to use for free. For years, California took unused upper basin water for its cities; now Arizona will put that water into the Central Arizona Project, and use it until, or if, the upper basin develops.

There is talk of the upper basin leasing its water to the lower basin. Entrepreneurs have attempted to figure out how such leases could occur without requiring too much alteration of the law. But it takes two to make a deal, and as of now, there isn't even one. The lower basin states see no reason to lease what they get for free; the upper basin states say their policy remains the development of water for use within their boundaries.

Instead of seeking deals with the lower basin, most upper basin energy is spent jockeying for control of the existing plumbing. The water establishment built upper basin reservoirs for agricultural, municipal, and industrial use. Their vision of western Colorado's and Wyoming's future was conventional: the conversion over time from agriculture to urban and industrial water uses, much as is occurring in the Phoenix-Tucson area.

It hasn't worked out that way in the upper basin. Western Colorado, whose mountains produce much of the river's water, lost its Great White Hope for water use when the oil shale industry collapsed. That industry was to use great amounts of water to convert rock into gasoline, and to water the cities that were to spring up to house the industry's workers.

Instead of oil shale, new uses have appeared — downhill and crosscountry skiing, fishing, hunting, rafting, hiking, and retirement — to compete for the Colorado River's water.

The recreation "industry" has always been in the rural West. It either searched out still undeveloped areas, and streams, or it has piggybacked on the reservoirs and regulated streamflows created by water development. Glen Canyon Dam, for example, has extended the river-running season through the Grand Canyon. In western Colorado, the Bureau just completed McPhee Dam on the Dolores River for farmers who now can't afford the water. But an infant rafting industry on that river would happily take all the water the Bureau will allocate to it.

Although environmental and recreation interests often coincide, they conflict on occasion. Snowmaking for downhill skiing takes water out of high mountain streams just when streamflow is at a minimium, and thus threatens fish. The effort to re-establish conditions appropriate to the mud- and warm-water loving endangered species in the Colorado has run into a sports fishing industry based on introduced, "exotic" varieties, such as rainbow trout.

These conflicts don't detract from the overall direction of the moment: Recreation and environmental interests are becoming influential on the Colorado River. Instream flow was crammed down the Wyoming water establishment's throat by the Wyoming Wildlife Federation. In Glenwood Springs, commercial rafters stopped a hydroelectric project that had the tax and water laws behind it, but which lacked the political support that once would have automatically rallied to it. The Sierra Club's attempt to use the courts to establish water rights in wilderness areas has stopped Colorado's wilderness bill for the moment, but may yield dividends when political negotiations begin.

The western Colorado ski town of Crested Butte, always out front in fighting for its interests, has taken on Aurora, which wants to divert water out of its valley. Ski resorts in the Colorado Rockies are now intensely involved in water matters, establishing water rights and building small, high-altitude reservoirs to make snow in the winter and water golf courses in the summer. They are engaged in the same kind of colonization of water that ranchers and farmers engaged in 80 years ago.

One is struck by the vitality of upper Colorado River water issues and by the number of people and interests involved in water. Ten years ago, water was an issue for the few. Today, contrary to the theory that harnessing a river leads in a totalitarian direction, it is a matter for the many.

The river is up for grabs because, although the plumbers did indeed reconstruct the river, they failed to secure the uses. Dams were built under the slogan, "use it or lose it." But dams are not uses, and once the reservoirs were in place, users descended on those reservoirs and the streamflows they controlled.

Is this revisionist history? Did the dam-builders, after all, know what they were doing? Under disguising slogans and catchwords, did they use federal funds to provide wisely for the future? Were Congressman Wayne Aspinall and his associates in Congress and in the Bureau visionaries, and not the porkbarrelers and villains they are painted in so many muckraking books?

There are no answers to the questions. We can only say that their work, accidentally or deliberately, left in place an adaptable system of plumbing. Today, various upper basin interests and economies are striving to use that plumbing in ways not written into the original plans. We can also say that those who plumbed the Colorado left a more flexible structure than those who plumbed the Columbia or Missouri.

Those who plumbed the river or inherited their mantles represent traditional interests and often fight the new uses. A Water Establishment is still present. But its powers are diluted; it must now negotiate rather than dictate solutions. And the negotiating table must be constantly fitted with new leaves to accommodate the expanding number of water interests.

21

With Reckless
Impetuosity

Rose Houk

The signs along Trail Ridge Road in Colorado's Rocky Mountain National Park say that the rivulet in the valley below is the Colorado River. It trickles through a meadow at the foot of the Never Summer Range with the torpor of September. It is hard to believe this is the same river whose frigid Grand Canyon waters downstream can capsize river-runners into fearsome rapids.

Ironically, this tiny new river has more water than it will in its final course, 1400 miles to the southwest. There, only a trickle of alkaline water remains to flow past Yuma, Arizona, through Mexico and, in wet years, into the Gulf of California.

At its headwaters, the Colorado is intercepted even before it earns the name "river." Grand Ditch, completed by settlers in 1892, is visible along the eastern flank of the Never Summer Range, depriving the newborn river below of melting snow. The ditch hustles water to the northeast across the Continental Divide, while the river flows southwest, toward the Gulf of California. The ditch is an 80-year-old symbol of the persistent fight for the river's water.

Major John Wesley Powell got his start here. His desire to explore the canyons of the Grand (the former name of the upper Colorado), the

Green, and the Colorado was stimulated by natural history expeditions in 1867 and 1868 in this high country. His base camp was at Middle Park Hot Springs, now the town of Hot Sulphur Springs that was a well-known watering place in Powell's time. The park, a flat, grassy high-altitude valley, is bounded by forests of spruce and fir. Everywhere there are mountains—Longs Peak to the northeast, the Gore Range to the southwest, and the Continental Divide and Berthoud Pass on the east. Powell's party heard the unearthly scream of mountain lions, and fought off torturous black gnats and mosquitoes.

The park has changed in many respects. A U.S. highway now runs through it and, down out of Middle Park, the Denver and Rio Grande tracks follow the river past Grand County's Hereford ranches and through a spectacular deep canyon. The gradient picks up and the river drops into a stretch now designated as "Gold Medal Waters" for its excellent trout fishing.

The river carves a 2000-foot-deep canyon along the northern end of the Gore Range, then works its way through the sagebrush plateaus above the small western Colorado towns of Burns and McCoy. At McCoy, the landscape is different. The rocks are sedimentary, flat-lying. Dark green pinon and juniper trees dot the red hillsides.

Kent and Donna Dannen

The Never Summer Range at the headwaters of the Colorado River, Rocky Mountain National Park, Colorado

A pair of raccoons waddle along the dirt road that follows the river, characters straight out of *Wind in the Willows*. They scoot down the bank as a car drives by, and then come back up and resume their journey along the roadside.

They are a reminder that the river provides a haven for all sorts of living creatures—there are fish that provide food for the raccoons, beaver chomping down the giant cottonwoods, and eagles, cranes, herons, and magpies that wouldn't be here were it not for the water, fish, cottonwoods, and willows.

The Blue River entered back at Kremmling; the Eagle River at Dotsero. The confluence of the Colorado and Interstate 70 also occurs at Dotsero, and to many this is the Colorado River. A sign warns that this tumultuous segment of river is "CLOSED TO BOATING." During the Pleistocene, about a million or so years ago, the Colorado River, swollen with the water of melted glaciers, began cutting Glenwood Canyon, slicing through the Paleozoic limestones and sandstones, down into the tough, old Precambrian granites.

Beyond Glenwood Canyon, after the Roaring Fork River has entered at Glenwood Springs, the Colorado neatly bisects the Grand Hogback, a sharp-crested ridge of steeply tilted rock. The guidebooks say this is where you officially leave the Rocky Mountains. This is the land of flat-topped mesas—Battlement and Grand mesas and the Bookcliffs—that stretch all the way to the Wasatch Mountains in Utah. The Rockies are behind, ahead lies the Colorado Plateau.

Here are the canyons that John Wesley Powell made famous. To many they are the Colorado River. The town of Grand Junction takes its name from the joining of the Gunnison and the Colorado, just as the river lazily skirts the northern end of the Uncompahgre Plateau. (See map on 154–155.) Ruby, Horsethief, and Westwater canyons ease you into the heartland, the canyonlands of Utah. Here the Green River, the Colorado's greatest tributary and arguably its true source, flows in just above Cataract Canyon in Canyonlands National Park.

Frederick Dellenbaugh, on Powell's second expedition down the Green and Colorado in 1871 and 1872, described the great confluence: "The two rivers blended gracefully on nearly equal terms, and the doubled volume started down with reckless impetuosity."

Powell was not content to call the whitewater here merely rapids, for it was not like anything he had experienced so far. These were cataracts, and one set now bears the infamous title of "The Big Drops." The river often goes on rampages in the spring, but it is stopped dead by the slack waters of Lake Powell. For now, the Colorado stops being a river.

Curving side canyons and sandbars. Springs dripping with maidenhair ferns. Datura flowers slowly opening at dusk. Painfully sweet

From roaring rapids to tepid puddle

Lee's Ferry in northernmost Arizona is the place where 15,000 people a year board motor and oar-driven rafts, kayaks, and dories to experience the Colorado River's grandest canyon.

They come to experience the river: its current, eddies, boils, calm stretches, and renowned rapids; its life: ducks scurrying ahead of the boat or bursting out of the water; flocks of those skillful flyers, the swallows, in pursuit of insect prey; pink blooms of the prolific tamarisk bushes at the water's edge; the canyon wren with its long descending call of solitude; the ring-tailed cat that checks out camp at night; a rattlesnake that momentarily takes the mind off a rapid being scouted from shore; the plastic-perfect and fluorescent-colored cactus flowers; the rare peregrine falcon or eagle flying between the canyon walls; the desert bighorn sheep somehow standing upright on slopes that appear impassable.

Adventurers on the river also experience the canyon rocks: the mostly flat-layered sedimentary rocks of various colors and hardnesses that arose from Paleozoic era seabeds and river floodplains; the older Precambrian schists and granites of the narrow inner gorge; the younger lavas that once dammed the canyon and formed a lake until the river could cut through the canyon walls and once again flow freely downstream.

And there are the river's side canyons: the blue-green waters of the Little Colorado River or lush Havasu Creek; waterfalls of every shape and size as streams crash down from the canyon rim to the river as much as 6000 feet below; swimming holes, a respite from temperatures reaching

Tourist atop Hoover Dam, which backs up giant Lake Mead

E.E. Hertzog, BuRec

over 110 degrees in the summertime; cottonwood trees and other plant life not found along the river itself because of periodic floods from Glen Canyon Dam; and with luck (good or bad, depending on where you are), a flash flood bringing brown water, mud, and rocks of every size crashing down toward the river and sometimes creating new rapids at the side stream's mouth.

Boaters emerge from the river at Diamond Creek and follow a dirt and rock road up the creek through the Hualapai Indian Reservation. Or they float another 50 miles into a bathtub called Lake Mead, which has twice as much water in it as flows down the entire Colorado River in an average year. Mead stands behind the oldest large manmade plug in the Colorado River, 50-year-old Hoover Dam. The lake is dotted with water skiers, sunbathers and fishermen; the dam crawls — both inside and out — with 300,000 people per year taking guided tours of it and its powerplant.

Grand Canyon's Inner Gorge

Philip Fradkin, in his book *A River No More*, describes the river below Hoover Dam as "a plumbing system of varying efficiency. Sometimes it gets stopped up and has to be relieved by dredging.... The water runs, for the most part, between channelized banks whose rock-ribbed sides have been stripped of all water-sucking plants." The water along this last stretch of the Colorado River is intensely used. Water is diverted to California's Imperial Valley and the metropolitan areas of southern California, both outside the Colorado River basin. Soon the river will also irrigate much of central Arizona and slake the thirst of city-dwellers in Phoenix and Tucson. And each dam in the series along this stretch of river is accompanied by an elecricity-producing powerplant. Recreation is also big here; Fradkin calls this part of the river "a tepid puddle for urban crowds."

The end of the story is perhaps the saddest part. In average rainfall years, the riverbed of the mighty Colorado dries up 10 or 20 miles before it reaches the Gulf of California, just after the last Mexican water diversion. So you can forget about standing atop the Continental Divide in Colorado's high country and expecting to be able to spit into both oceans. Perhaps your eastward spit will make it to the Gulf of Mexico. Your westward spit may irrigate an orchard or beanfield in the high country, or lettuce in the Imperial Valley. Perhaps it will be tunneled back under the Divide to the Denver area, or maybe it will evaporate from those big bathtubs in the southwestern deserts. It could end up in a coffee cup in Los Angeles. But unless it's a wet year, there's one thing you can be sure of: It won't make it to the Gulf of California.

— *Mary Moran*

sand verbena. Soaring sandstone cliffs. Many have written of the incredible magic that pervades this southeastern Utah canyon country, that has as its heart the Colorado River.

Across the border in Arizona lies Glen Canyon Dam, and below it, Lees Ferry, where the Paria River quietly flows in from the west. The ferry is a topographic and historic landmark, designated for many reasons as the river's mile zero. It is the only place for the next 225 miles where you can drive down to the river's edge and stick your big toe into the 50 degree waters of the Colorado River.

22

Sharing Water with the Colossus of the North

Jose Trava

66 Don't get apprehensive, Juan . . . Look! Can you see all that dust in the distance? There . . . down the road. Do you see that brownish spot? Yeah, that's El Rio . . . That's where we're heading.

"You will see, Juan . . . You will see! We are going to be rich, really rich. Look, all of them are virgin lands. They are only mud and dust right now, but with a little bit of work, they will become green and beautiful . . . and productive. Twenty years from now, El Rio will be flourishing. You will see, Juan . . . we all will see it."

At the turn of the century, Mexican pioneers came from the west, from the played-out mines in the mountains along Baja California's Pacific coast, to settle what is now the Mexicali Valley. They had heard of this isolated region, and they put their hopes on "nobody" land— land free for the taking. Even the sight of this desolate floodplain of the Colorado River, near the Gulf of California, couldn't dim their enthusiasm.

One account from February 1901 describes the early settlement: "That morning I found myself in the middle of those new lands, facing a new sun and new people from El Rio. Close to our camp there was a marsh and on its surroundings other families also settled and built small huts under the mesquite's shadows. That was the way El Rio, the town, was born. No planification was made, nobody gave any kind of order to build it.

"Labor work, provided by the Americans at the other side (of the fence) made it possible for the town to grow. It was born very, very close to the canal that divided the United States from Mexico . . . It was like a flower from the wilderness — defenseless, in the hands of the Lord."

It is extraordinary that, until the turn of this century, the mouth of a major U.S. river should have been occupied by only 1200 Cucapah Indians. But the Colorado River delta was no place for a New Orleans or New York. Its approach was up the narrow, isolated Gulf of California; it was guarded by huge mud flats, fluctuating river flows that could ground vessels in a moment, an unstable riverbed that shifted more often than the Mississippi, and very rough water called tidal bores — caused by the interaction between the gulf's tide and the river's flow — that could and did sink boats that navigated the lower Colorado.

When development finally came to this hot and barren place, it came in a rush, on both sides of the border. In 1902, El Rio was renamed Mexicali. Across the border, its sister American city got a sister name: Calexico.

A form of civilization had preceded Juan and the other settlers. The "nobody" lands already belonged to Don Guillermo Andrade, a Mexican from the state of Sonora. In 1877, he had been granted the rights to colonize 300,000 hectares (a hectare is 2.47 acres) within the delta. Such concessions were common during the dictatorship of General Porfirio Diaz, who was driven from power at the start of the Mexican Revolution in 1911.

Plans to irrigate the Arizona side of the border began in 1891, but foundered. In 1899, the California Development Company decided that California's Imperial Valley, the northern extension of the Mexicali Valley, should be irrigated. To reach it, water had to pass through Andrade's lands and a deal was struck. In June 1901, irrigation water flowed into the Imperial Valley by way of Mexico. A month later, 6000 acres were under cultivation.

The Cucapah Indians had moved up into the mountains, but one of them, Dos de Bastos, would come to Mexicali and, being invited to drink coffee and alcohol at Don Ramon Zumaya's grocery store, would tell how the world looked to him:

"All of this, everything, will be water again very soon . . . because the soul of the Colorado River will look for his old and cherished home in the salty sea of the north . . . and also because our Cucapah Great Elder has announced that some day the river body will follow his soul;

that's why we Indians still live in the mountains and watch the white men fight for the lands . . . which belong to Cucapahs . . ."

In spring 1905, the soul of the river spoke. Engineering works on the diversion dam—the dam that pushed the Colorado out of its bed and into a canal leading to the Imperial Valley—gave way, and spilled water over the land. Uncontrolled, the river hit Mexicali, and total destruction threatened. Christmas 1905 was tragic. Almost all 50 houses in Mexicali were abandoned; people fled to Calexico.

The floods returned in 1906, and in January 1907, "A general feeling of distress go on everybody in the valley." People on both sides of the border had good reason for fear. All efforts to recapture the river failed. For two years, the Colorado, untamed wreaked havoc.

It was no surprise. As anyone who has visited the Grand Canyon or southern Utah could guess, the Colorado carries an enormous amount of silt. Historically, much of it ended up in the Colorado River delta, lifting whatever bed the water was flowing in at the moment until the river was forced to change course. A single day's supply of water to the valley had enough silt, according to Frank Waters' *The Colorado*, to build a levee 20 feet high, 20 feet wide and a mile long. The river filled in canals in a moment. It dumped mountains of silt at diversion points. It toyed with the toy structures the would-be diverters had built.

Finally, in 1905, it got serious. The river, in part due to operating and engineering mistakes, quit its built-up, elevated path to the gulf and headed via old river channels to the inland Salton Sea, in the north of the Mexicali-Imperial Valley. The irrigation company made several attempts to push the river out of its new channel, but the dams and levees it built were pushed aside by the river.

Farmers in the Imperial Valley feared the sea would grow indefinitely and drown their fertile land. It was then that President Theodore Roosevelt both exerted pressure and made promises of federal payment to Edward Harriman, president of the Southern Pacific Railroad Company, if the firm would recapture the river. In response, the railroad galvanized its resources, giving track priority to rock and gravel trains throughout the system. Frank Waters writes:

"Two railroad trestles of 90-foot piling were built across the break. Across these were run trains dumping rock into the river faster than it could be swept away. That was all there was to it.

"But to achieve this, the Los Angeles and Tucson divisions of the Southern Pacific and 12,000 miles of main-line traffic were tied up for three weeks . . . Rock was rushed in from the mountains near Patagonia, Arizona, 485 miles away, and from quarries on the Santa Fe and Salt Lake roads. Special trains carrying piling and timbers from New Orleans were given right-of-way. Dumping began. Never before had rock been dumped so fast: 3000 cars of rock totaling 80,000 cubic yards in 15 days. The whole river was raised bodily 11 feet."

It was a contest between the Southern Pacific's ability to carry in dirt and rock and the Colorado's ability to carry it away. On February 10, 1907, the railroad won and the river was pushed back into its old trough to the gulf. (Harriman never did get any help from Congress with his $3 million bill.)

People were jubilant. The flood menace had ended for the moment. On the open and still wet fields, a great Mass was offered.

Unfortunately, the land the Mexicans were praying on was not theirs, or even Andrade's. It now belonged to the Colorado River Land Company, a subsidiary of the California-Mexico Land and Cattle Company, which was founded by American Harry Chandler in August 1902. The company had come into possession of 350,000 hectares (875,000 acres) in the delta by paying $173,000 to Andrade.

Soon the pioneer-settlers were told: "In the name of the Colorado River Land Company and due to the fact that all of the land of the northern part of Baja California known as the 'Andrade Concession' is now in our possession, take notice you must move out of the area within two months upon receiving this notification . . ."

All 400 pioneers who had settled on "nobody's" land, the promised land, now felt the force of capitalism's modern machine. In a very few years, the frontier had vanished and a new era begun: that of bold American investors who, through a series of land and water speculations, became the most powerful and richest men in southern California.

The area changed and grew under this new order. In 1910, Don Gustavo Terrazas, first magistrate of the city of Mexicali, ordered a census: 462 people were counted, of whom 294 were men and 168 women. There were another 1417 people in the surrounding area, including 273 Cucapah Indians. Los Algodones, 50 miles east of Mexicali, had 195 people, most working men.

In 1912, cotton was grown for the first time in the Mexicali Valley. By 1916, 26,600 acres were harvested by the Colorado River Land Company for a $1 million profit. It was the Golden Epoch. Between 1915 and 1930, cotton harvests increased; in 1919, at the end of World War I, profits were over $18 million. The population was also changing. By 1915, more than 10,000 Chinese "coolies" had arrived, the majority doing farm work.

By 1920, Mexicali was flourishing, but agriculture had little to do with it. As a result of Prohibition, cabarets, casinos, and canteens proliferated. Americans, Chinese, Greeks, Japanese, Spanish, Italians and French were the owners of lusty places where Americans, escaping the "dry law," spent enormous amounts of money. On July 23,

1923, Jack B. Tenney, a young pianist in one of the casinos, made the city famous by composing *The Mexicali Rose* for a dancer he was in love with.

Meanwhile, the Colorado River Land Company had hit on a way to increase its profits: The lands were given on lease to users who had to hand over 20 percent of their harvest to the company; the remaining 80 percent went to traders specified by the company. Lessors were chosen from illegal aliens—mainly Chinese, Japanese and Hindustani; Mexicans were excluded.

In the Imperial Valley, a few hundred yards to the north, settlers had transformed themselves into dependable farmers who owned and understood their land and water. But the dominance of the Colorado River Land Company severely hindered development of the Mexicali Valley by Mexicans. The company had converted the region into an immense hacienda, in which Mexicans, when lucky enough, worked almost as slaves in their own motherland.

The system went on for years. Then, on January 27, 1937, determined campesinos, peasants from different parts of the Mexicali Valley, peacefully invaded the company's empire. When President Lazaro Cardenas got the news, he summoned the campesinos to Mexico City and promised a solution "as soon as possible."

Their leaders were skeptical. Earlier attempts at land reform had been beaten back. For example, under the new constitution, only Mexican citizens could own land. But the law wasn't enforced. Back in 1929, a woman named Felipa Velazquez had helped organize an agrarian reform committee and claimed land. The Mexican government arrested all the campesino leaders and sent them to Marias Island, a federal prison.

Repression didn't stop the push for land. Due to the Great Depression of 1929 in the United States, many Mexican workers returned to Mexico. In 1936, the Mexican government under Presidente Cardenas forced the Colorado River Land Company to agree that all of the firm's 258,000 hectares would eventually be occupied by campesinos. The government would compensate the firm.

The company was too rich and proud to comply. During the next six months, only 426 hectares were assigned to campesinos. So in March 1937, a letter from Presidente Cardenas was given to astonished campesino leaders. It gave them the right to settle on 4120 hectares of company land. Soon after, more permission came. The hacienda was shattered. A year later, the land reform was extended when Mexico expropriated the property of foreign oil companies.

It took until 1937 for the Mexican government to help its own people in the Mexicali Valley get control of the land. By comparison, U.S. efforts to aid those who settled in neighboring Imperial Valley

E. E. Hertzog, BuRec

Lettuce harvest in the Imperial Valley

had begun when Roosevelt got the Southern Pacific to control the rampaging Colorado.

The recapture of the Colorado didn't solve all problems. It was still an "overhead" river, riding a channel several hundred feet higher than the Imperial farmland, and carrying an enormous amount of silt. Canals regularly silted up and another runaway flood was not out of the question. Continued problems had prompted the U.S. settlers to form the Imperial Irrigation District in 1911, and to purchase Southern Pacific's facilities and water rights in 1916. (The railroad had gotten control by infusing capital into the irrigation company as it struggled to control the flooding Colorado.)

The farmers' next step, for security reasons, was to seek an "all-American" canal — one north of the border. But the Bureau of Reclamation said such a canal would be impractical without an upriver dam to control flooding and to capture silt. During the same period, Los Angeles was seeking a power supply. A large dam would provide both electricity and flood and silt control.

But there was political opposition to the plugging of the Colorado River to provide electricity and water for California. The six other states on the river feared that California, whose growth far exceeded their own, would drain the river dry of both water and hydropower.

The result was the Colorado River Compact of 1922, allocating water between the three lower basin states (California, Arizona and Nevada) and the four upper basin states (Wyoming, Colorado, New Mexico, and Utah). (See map on 154–155.) Under the impression that the river ran 18 million acre-feet a year, it gave 7.5 million acre-feet a year to each basin. We now know the compact was negotiated during a wet period, and that the river actually averages about 14 million acre-feet.

With the compact more or less out of the way (Arizona refused to ratify it), Congress authorized construction of Boulder Dam, now Hoover Dam, in 1928. It and its reservoir, Lake Mead, were dedicated in 1935. Now the river was physically and legally under control. Excavation for the All-American Canal began in 1934; delayed by floods and an earthquake, it was supplying all the Imperial Valley's needs by 1942.

Mexico was made nervous by U.S. development of the Colorado. Attempts to divide the river's waters internationally had begun in 1912, and occurred sporadically after that. In 1939, the Rio Colorado Irrigation District was established in the Mexicali Valley, giving farmers an organized voice. Soon after, in July 1941, the Mexican ambassador in Washington presented the United States with a draft of a treaty.

The United States was eager to keep Mexico as a war-time ally, and a treaty was signed in 1944. It assigned 1.5 million acre-feet a year of the Colorado's flow to Mexico, without cutting the allocations to the seven states, and created the International Boundary Water Commission to administer it.

The quality of the 1.5 million acre-feet is not mentioned in the treaty. This stemmed from the way negotiators convinced their respective governments to sign. The U.S. Senate was told that the Mexicans would only get salty irrigation drainage that was heading for Mexico anyway. Mexican negotiators told their country that the United States had to deliver "good quality" water.

The treaty took effect in November 1945. In 1948, Presa Morelos, a diversion dam in Mexico a mile south of the border near Yuma, Arizona, began operating. An "All-Mexican" canal stretch was completed soon after. The Mexicali Valley was again a land of promise. It had a secure source of water, fertile land and a growing population – 124,000 people in 1950, with half of them under age 21. Half of the population lived in Mexicali.

For the next 10 years, peace and goodwill reigned. Even though the Colorado River averaged only 14 million acre-feet a year, there was enough water because the upper basin states had not developed the agriculture or cities to use their water. The average delivery to Mexico at the boundary was 4.24 million acre-feet a year. Quality was acceptable, too. Total dissolved solids at Morelos Dam averaged 900 parts per million – the same as upstream across the border at Imperial Dam.

It couldn't last. In October 1961, at the end of the cotton season, water delivered to Mexico dropped to a minimum, as usual. But that water contained an incredible 2500 parts per million of salinity. What had happened?

To solve a high water table problem in Arizona's Wellton-Mohawk Valley, a small irrigation area east of Yuma, the Bureau of Reclamation had drilled more than 60 wells. Without warning to Mexico, those wells began lifting 350 cubic feet per second of drain water containing 6000 ppm of salt that had been washed out of the soil by irrigation. The pumping saved the area's crops from dying a salty, water-logged death.

This salty drain water was dumped into the Gila River near its confluence with the Colorado. To make things worse, this occurred just when Lake Powell in Utah started filling behind Glen Canyon Dam, cutting the water available for dilution. The situation could go on for 25 years.

The Mexicali farmers were furious, and the Mexican government argued that the treaty had been violated. The United States pointed out that the treaty didn't discuss water quality. Even worse, the United States turned paternal, offering to send technicians to teach Mexican farmers how to deal with salinity problems. Mexico was offended.

Then began years of negotiations, first between President John F. Kennedy and Presidente Lopez Mateos, and later between Lyndon Johnson and Lopez Mateos. A temporary solution led to construction in 1965 of a canal that let drain water from the Wellton-Mohawk Valley bypass Mexico's Morelos Dam. Research during this time showed salinity was important. Damages could reach $3.7 million a year on the 500,000 acres irrigated in the area, or $370 a year for the average 50-acre farm.

Things got worse for Mexicali's campesinos in 1966, when the Gila South District in the United States began discharging salty drainage into the Colorado River. The water upstream of Morelos, even without the Wellton-Mohawk flow, was 1300 ppm instead of the desired 900 ppm. Adding insult to injury, the salt water from the Gila South District was counted as part of Mexico's share of the Colorado. The dispute during the late 1960s focused on what was "Colorado River water." Mexico said water pumped out of the ground by irrigation districts seeking to lower water tables and carry off dissolved salt was not Colorado River water. The United States said it was.

Meanwhile, Mexicali kept growing; it reached 396,000, a 219 percent increase from 1950, in 1970. The possible loss of the valley's irrigated lands to saline water horrified Mexican officials.

After further fruitless negotiations, Mexico came up with a new argument: According to its reading of the 1922 Colorado River Compact, Mexico was the eighth water user, with the seven states. Thus,

Mexico should be allowed the same benefits as its neighbors. It was ridiculous, Mexican negotiators said, that Imperial Valley farmers had 850 ppm water while, a few thousand feet away, campesinos were stunting their crops with 1300 ppm water.

The solution, however, lay not with Mexican arguments, but with the American political process. 1972 was an election year and sympathy for Mexico was building. In March, during an annual meeting held in Mexico City, the National Wildlife Federation supported Mexico's position. In May, at the U.S.A. – Mexico Twelfth Inter-Parliamentary meeting in New Orleans, U.S. Senator Mike Mansfield of Montana asked for a non-litigious, practical, quick solution. A few days later, Senator Hubert Humphrey, campaigning for the presidency, said that "based on pure ethical reasons, the U.S. government should bring to an end the salinity controversy."

On June 15, 1972, Mexican Presidente Luis Echeverria spoke to the U.S. Congress: "Imperial and Mexicali valleys belong both to the same basin, that of the mighty Colorado River; the only possible

Laguna Dam, below the Imperial Dam on the Colorado River. The All-American Canal is in the upper left-hand corner of the photo.

interpretation of the 1944 treaty is that riparian nations should work out solutions based on sincerity and equity . . . We can't understand why the same spirit and imagination the United States deploys to unravel intricate problems with his enemies are not used to solve very simple matters with his friends. . ."

Negotiations began again, but now the pressure was toward compromise. After false starts, agreement was reached in August 1973. It guaranteed Mexico a water quality within 121 ppm of that delivered to the Imperial Valley.

Presidente Echeverria called Minute 242 "a triumph of reason and human rights; an honest reward for our tenacious diplomats and . . . a promising landmark for our future relations with the United States." It was a victory for understanding and goodwill. It became a celebrated affair, an example of cordial relations between two neighboring nations.

As an agricultural engineer assigned to the region since 1977, I have learned that the solution to the salinity problem was almost equivalent to the 1937 assault by campesinos on the Colorado River

Land Company's land: both represented crucial turning points in the region's history.

For Mexico and the Mexicali Valley, it was a matter of survival. Land productivity was in jeopardy and population was building. For the years to come, a solid and stable situation was needed. Without it there could be no investment in agriculture.

In addition, municipal uses are increasing. At present, 83,000 acre-feet per year of Colorado River water go to municipal use in the Mexicali Valley. Another 25,000 acre-feet are being transferred to Tijuana, on the Pacific coast. As the urban trend continues, farmers will be under pressure to grow more crops with less water. They will need both research and financial support.

I think they will succeed. They will struggle, as always, but new generations, as tenacious as their ancestors, will find a way out of their troubles.

23

The Bureau's Rube Goldberg Machines

Paul Krza

The Soviet Union is known for its virgin lands program: Soviet functionaries, by coercion or persuasion, convince people to settle in Siberia. It is less well known that the United States has also had such programs. In the 1950s, for example, U.S. Bureau of Reclamation officials convinced farmers that they and the agency could make the desert of southwest Wyoming bloom.

According to farmer Eugene Hodder, making the desert bloom wasn't all the Bureau cracked it up to be. The farm he settled on did not live up to advance billing. In its mid-1950s pitch, the Bureau made the area sound almost like paradise, and in fact, the land that caught Hodder's eye was called Eden Valley, near the tiny towns of Eden and Farson. Today, an older, wiser Hodder says: "They definitely flowered it up. I thought it was a good deal."

So good that he packed up his family and moved from the rich, dark soils of their Utah home to the new federal promised land alongside the Big Sandy River. There, over three decades, he picked up an education on farming the coarse, rapidly draining soils of the high-altitude desert.

Hodder was one of the pioneers in the Bureau's twilight zone of marginal agriculture—the development of "virgin land for home-

Stan Rasmussen, BuRec

Water flowed from this hole in Fontenelle Dam during September 1965

steading." He qualified as a "settler" because he was judged to have "traits of character and industry that include honesty, temperate habits, thrift, and bona fide intent to engage in farming as an occupation."

Those weren't enough when pitted against the soil and climate of southwestern Wyoming, and 30 years later any visions of a blooming desert have wilted. Outside, the winter fog settles around a modest house and trailer he and his son James call home. Inside, in a living room that doubles as a bedroom, the Hodders say they would jump at the chance to sell out. Farming is in trouble everywhere, but things are really tough on its edge, in Eden. "If we knew a way out, we'd be gone," the father says. "We're not here for the money," laughs James.

The Eden Valley, where blazing orange and purple sunsets splash on the nearby Wind River Mountains, may be "a good place to raise kids," James says, "but you have to be pretty dedicated to stay in agriculture here."

The Hodders are the rule rather than the exception. The Bureau's irrigation project serves 84 farm families; 79 are part-time farmers who work in Rock Springs or in trona mines to support themselves and their farms. They've sacrificed to stay with their farms. Sadly, the nation would be better off economically if they were to take a walk.

No one would blame them. Experts say there is only a 50-50 chance that the growing season in the 6500-foot-high valley will last 85 days in any given year. As a result, only small grain crops, alfalfa, barley, and oats can be grown, and those just barely. In Utah, Hodder could expect six to 10 tons an acre. In Eden, the range is one to three tons.

Two small reservoirs impound snowmelt from the Wind River Mountains. The Eden Valley farmers use it to virtually flood their lands. Unfortunately, the sandy, porous soil must be flooded frequently because it doesn't hold moisture well. The frequent waterings wash down through the porous ground removing both nutrients and the salt that is left over from the time when the area was a lake bottom.

The economic damage to the nation comes because irrigation of the 15,000 acres the 84 families farm adds 133,000 tons of salt per year to the Big Sandy. From there, the salt flows to the Green River and then to the Colorado River. By the time the water is diverted into California or Mexico, natural and irrigation sources such as Eden Valley have put 9 million tons of salt in the water. That salt causes $490 million in damages to crops and cities in California and Mexico. (Salt from Eden Valley is responsible for $7.3 million of that damage.)

To reduce the damage to crops in such places as the Imperial Valley of California and Mexico, the federal government is paying for a variety of desalinization projects. Some land that contributes salt is productive, and worth saving. But the cheapest way to remove Eden Valley's salt would be to buy up the farms and let them go back to sage. The feds proposed just that, but it ran counter to Wyoming state government policy of preserving agriculture.

So the U.S. Soil Conservation Service now wants the farmers to switch from flood irrigation to sprinklers; they would put less water on the land and leach less salt out of the soil. The farmers are willing, if the feds help pay for the sprinklers and for the extra cost involved in operating them.

Although the Eden Valley project looks like a perpetual burden on both the settlers and the taxpayer, it has performed a valuable service

Paul Krza

James and Eugene Hodder at their farm in the Eden Valley

as a deterrent. Roughly 30 miles to the west along the Green River where similar lands lie, sagebrush still grows. Farmers like Hodder were to till 60,000 acres of reclaimed desert there, and a dam was built, complete with outlet works and canals. But in the mid-1960s, reality caught up with the Bureau's dream. So the canals trail off into the desert, and the leaking dam doesn't even hold water. Fontenelle Reservoir's emptiness is either an act of nature, according to the Bureau, or an act of poor engineering. The fact that 60,000 acres of desert land aren't in marginal agriculture, contributing hundreds of thousands of tons of salt to the Colorado, is a result of the warning put out by the Eden Valley project.

To be fair to the Bureau, it hadn't wanted to build Eden Valley. In 1939, the Bureau and another agency studied the Eden project and both painted a "very bleak picture" of its chances for success, according to Professor David Kathka, a Western Wyoming College history professor. The studies were reinforced by experience: Three privately funded irrigation ventures had already failed in the valley.

But powerful Wyoming Democratic Senator Joseph C. O'Mahoney threatened to go directly to the Secretary of Interior unless Bureau officials changed their minds. O'Mahoney got his way. The senator, who served for 26 years in the Senate, also pushed for Fontenelle and the associated Seedskadee project to irrigate 60,000 acres of desert on either side of the Green River downstream of Fontenelle.

On Seedskadee, the Bureau was in accord with O'Mahoney. Bureau engineers, used to seeing water turn desert land green and productive, and apparently unmindful of the different soil and climate of western Wyoming, pushed ahead. The agency got extravagant support in Rock Springs for the project. A 1955 newspaper editorial said the Upper Colorado River Project, of which Seedskadee was a part, would help develop "vast uranium deposits," irrigate land the United States would "desperately need" in 25 years, create jobs, aid the national defense, and "make America stronger, better, richer and more beautiful."

The project was pushed forward by economic developments in southwest Wyoming. The Union Pacific Railroad, after converting its engines from coal to diesel, closed coal mines at Rock Springs and trimmed rail crews at Green River. An Appalachian-like depression gripped the area.

That depression coincided with heady times for the Bureau, fresh from a series of technical triumphs. According to Kathka, who has studied the era, agency officials were touring the globe, pushing reclamation as the key to "feeding the world and fighting communism."

With local pressures reinforcing O'Mahoney's work in Congress, the project got funding, and in June 1961 work began on Fontenelle. It was to be a 137-foot-high earthen dam stretching about a mile across the wide Green River Valley, 59 miles northwest of the city of Green River. It is the only dam in Wyoming on the Green, the largest tributary of the Colorado.

Bids were taken, the jobless hired and heavy equipment put to work. But a few months later, the project began to ravel. The first blow came from a budding industry. Trona, or soda ash, producers were worried that irrigation water would seep into their underground mines and ruin the water-soluble mineral. So the project was scaled back.

A year later, in May 1962, as workers were pouring concrete for the irrigation canals, the Commissioner of Reclamation halted the irrigation part of the project. O'Mahoney's Seedskadee project had been stopped by O'Mahoney's Eden Valley Project.

Congressional hearings on Eden and another project on the Wind River Indian Reservation in central Wyoming (see Chapter 19) "brought to light the serious financial and economic problems encountered by farmers on these high-altitude projects," the stop order said. The 1939 warnings had reached Washington.

But work on Fontenelle Dam went on; it was finished and apparently ready to hold water by late summer 1964. Trouble appeared immediately in the form of suspicious seeps downstream. The dam held the record snowmelt of 1965 only until September 3, when a Bureau engineer's nightmare appeared: a "wet spot" on the dam embankment. By the next morning, the next worst Bureau experience to Teton Dam was developing: a "near failure" of Fontenelle.

"We saw the harsh reality of the flowing wound on the downstream face," Bureau Regional Director David Crandall recalled later. A quick drain, made quicker by dumping water into the irrigation canal works that led out into the desert, averted a break and the flooding of the downstream town of Green River.

Anyone who has visited a Bureau dam will remember the impression of control, of cleanliness, of humming turbines, of unflappable competence. The Bureau attempted to portray the same infallibility during the Fontenelle crisis. Over the several days it took to drain the reservoir, Crandall went on the radio to tell the locals not to worry. Agency "technical engineers who really know what they are doing" were keeping close tabs on the situation. Moreover, it was not a situation of the Bureau's making. It was all Mother Nature's fault:

"The leak problem at Fontenelle is not, I can assure you, the result of a technical inadequacy," Crandall told his radio listeners. "When you deal with the forces of nature, you sometimes encounter the unexpected."

With the reservoir empty, the Bureau repaired the hole, replacing a 345-foot section of dam, and dumping 126 railcars of cement into the leaky rock foundation to stop the seeps that had created the growing hole.

The fix seemed to work, and the dam began storing water uneventfully, but also without any real purpose since there was no irrigation project. In 1970, Fontenelle got its first customer. Oregon-based Pacific Power and Light Company used one quarter of the reservoir's capacity, 60,000 acre-feet a year, to cool its giant 2000-megawatt Jim Bridger Power Plant near Rock Springs. Sixteen years later, that remains the only use.

Meanwhile, the reservoir continued to seep, and in 1982 a Bureau inspection team judged it to be in "poor" condition. The determination came during a heavy water year on the upper Colorado River basin. Fontenelle was brimful, and the town of Green River was nervous. Bureau engineers said there was no danger.

The agency also announced an expensive plan to re-repair the ailing dam — this time with "state-of-the-art" construction techniques. A thin concrete "wall" was to be inserted inside the earthen embankment for $52 million. But Washington had changed since Senator O'Mahoney got free dams for his constituents. Wyoming was asked to foot part of the bill. The Legislature appropriated $5.3 million and Congress approved the project. It will take at least three

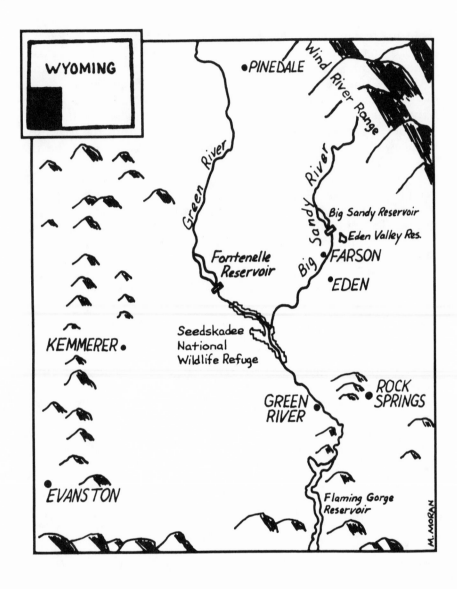

summers to install the wall, which means three more nervous years for Green River.

Why not simply open the dam gates and let the river run as if it were not there? First, because of the "use it or lose it" doctrine. Wyoming officials see the 240,000 acre-foot reservoir as a key to hanging onto the state's share of Colorado River water. Common sense says that only 60,000 acre-feet are being used; water sense says Wyoming is using 240,000 acre-feet.

Second, there is no constituency for abandoning the dam, even among environmentalists. Just downstream is the Seedskadee Wildlife Refuge, prime duck habitat. It was created to make up for the drowning of the river habitat at Fontenelle. If Fontenelle were abandoned, there would be no dependable flow of water to maintain the refuge's wetlands.

The result of "water sense" is that land in the Eden Valley continues to pour salt into the river and $52 million is being spent to repair a dam that, given the depressed nature of Wyoming's economy, has little foreseeable future use. Just downstream of Fontenelle, the ducks in the Seedskadee Refuge are happy. Farther downstream, in Green River, the residents are hoping the upper Colorado won't have a heavy water year until the dam is repaired.

24

What Size Shoe Does an Acre-Foot Wear?

Ed Quillen

Many people have questions about water. They wonder why water diversions are not diverting, why it is morally offensive to leave water flowing in a stream, why water and sex are closely related. The glossary that follows answers those questions, as well as many questions that have never been asked, and which there is no reason to answer.

Acre-foot: The amount of water required to cover one acre, which is about the size of a football field, or 0.40468564 hectare, to a depth of one foot, about the length of a football shoe, or 30.48 centimeters — that is, about 325,848.882718339 gallons or 1,233.43773084702 steres. Most popularly explained as the amount of water an average family of four uses in one year, but this definition is too fluid, only in desert regions is it appropriate.

For example, in a wet state like Minnesota, the average family of four consumes only 0.44 acre-feet of treated water in a year, and in Oregon, it's all of 0.34 acre-feet. But in dry Colorado, it's 0.93 acre-feet; arid Wyoming, 0.96 acre-feet; thirsty Arizona, 0.99; desert Nevada, 1.12; and parched Utah, 2.46. These dull figures (given the topic, they can't be dry statistics) demonstrate that treated water is unlike other commodities: The less gasoline there is available, the

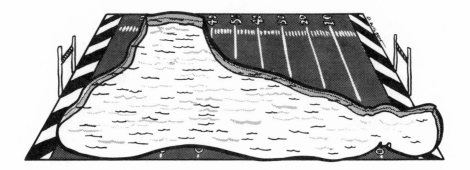

less people consume, but the less water there is, the more people consume.

Augmentation: In standard arithmetic, to augment means to add something. For instance, $200,000 augmented by $200,000 comes to $400,000. Water arithmetic is more complicated. Assume that a basin has an annual water production of 400,000 acre-feet. A metropolis across the mountain range desires to take 300,000 acre-feet. To placate the basin residents, the metropolis builds an "augmentation reservoir" with a capacity of 50,000 acre-feet. Before augmentation, the basin residents had 400,000 acre-feet. After augmentation, they have 100,000 acre-feet. Thus 400,000 augmented by 50,000 comes to 100,000. For more insight into the logic upon which water arithmetic is based, see Charles Dodgson's influential works, *Through the Looking Glass* and *Alice's Adventure in Wonderland.*

Beneficial use: Any use of water which (1) takes water out of a natural channel, and (2) benefits a bank account. Thus courts have held that keeping water in rivers so that fish might swim in it is not a beneficial use, whereas using the water to carry silt into collection impoundments (often called reservoirs) is a beneficial use.

California: A mythical land, first described in the 15th-century Spanish romance, *Las Sergas de Esplandian,* by Garcia Ordonez de Montalva. This California was populated only by women, ruled by virgin Queen Califa, and contained vast quantities of gold and pearls. In current mythology, California is the place to which water flows and then vanishes utterly, as in "If we don't use it, then California will take it." The only way to prevent this awful waste of upper basin resources is to allow the water to evaporate from Denver lawns and Utah reservoirs.

CFS: See Cubic feet per second. Colorado writer Lewis Newell once discovered an interesting similarity between the CFS and the

UFO; many people believe in both, but no reliable witness has ever seen either.

Compact: An agreement, such as the famous Colorado River Compact, concerning deliveries of water between states. One of the most curious must be the Colorado-Kansas Compact. In 1984, Colorado erred and allowed the Arkansas River to flow into Kansas for the first time in years; normally, the riverbed by Holly is as dry as a Baptist wedding because Colorado grabs every last drop. Unaccustomed to seeing water in the river, Kansas promptly responded with a lawsuit.

Conservancy district: In standard English, conservancy refers to the preservation of natural resources. In water English, a conservancy district is a legal device for destroying fisheries, riparian habitats, wetlands, and indigenous populations.

Cubic feet per second: See Cusec.

Cusec: See CFS.

Diversion: An entertainment. For instance, a popular metropolitan diversion is to dry up high mountain valleys by piping water to the cities below. Then the metropolis invites immigrants by promoting both its ample water supply and its proximity to pristine mountain valleys with sparkling fishing streams.

Irrigation: The construction of vast works (dams, tunnels, canals, and so on) at public expense in order to produce surplus expense in order to produce surplus agricultural commodities, which are then purchased and stored at public expense.

Myth: A fictitious belief widely held by influential people. Water myths have had an important effect on Western settlement and public policy. To wit, dozens of explorers died searching for the Rio Buenaventura, a mythical water route from the Midwest to the Pacific Ocean. Thousands of sodbusters faced starvation because they believed the myth that "rain follows the plow" or that "the smoke from locomotives makes it rain." Current myths include "water development assures prosperity" and "there is unappropriated water available in the Gunnison River for the city of Aurora, 200 miles and three mountain ranges away."

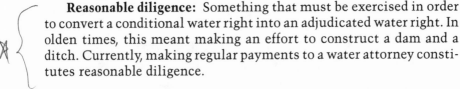

Reasonable diligence: Something that must be exercised in order to convert a conditional water right into an adjudicated water right. In olden times, this meant making an effort to construct a dam and a ditch. Currently, making regular payments to a water attorney constitutes reasonable diligence.

Reclamation: In standard English, "reclamation" means to return something to a former use. In water English, "reclamation" means converting land that has always been desert into farmland, a use it never had.

Salinity: A measure of water degradation related to the concentration of sodium ions; the chief characteristic of water delivered by the United States to Mexico to fulfill treaty obligations.

Sex: Often compared to water in light of certain similarities: (1) Many believe in the doctrine of "first in time, first in right." (2) Many believe you must "use it or lose it." (3) Nobody ever has enough.

Uphill: The natural direction that Western water flows, providing there is money uphill.

Water right: A property right to certain quantities of water in certain locations, depending upon the use of the water and the priority date of the water right. Water rights are either very valuable, because men have given their lives in battles over water rights, or else of little value, because, unlike other forms of real and personal property, water rights are not taxed.

Windygap: Windy Gap is the site of a reservoir and pumping plant near Granby, Colorado, constructed by six cities on the other side of the Rockies. When the six cities began the project, they said they needed additional municipal water supplies because they would otherwise buy up Colorado-Big Thompson water shares to slake the thirsts of their growing populations, and thus dry up productive farmland. Then the cities turned around and assigned much of their Windy Gap water for cooling the Rawhide Electric Power Plant near Fort Collins, claiming that they needed the electricity for their municipal utilities. However, all of the Rawhide electric production is being sold to Public Service Company; the customers in those cities have yet to receive so much as a kilowatt from Rawhide. Now some of the cities are trying to sell their Windy Gap water, saying that they really didn't need the water in the first place. Thus a new verb has been coined. To "windygap" is to deceive, plunder resources, and waste money on a colossal scale, as in "We never thought we'd get that project approved by those rural county commissioners, but we windygapped it right through, after we persuaded them that it was for their own good if we took their water."

25

Night Watch

C. L. Rawlins

Alone, in a gray boat on a black lake, cold water cupped in bedrock above 10,000 feet. No moon, no wind; high, thin clouds and scattered stars. I row with short, even strokes and the boat rises and dips with the movement of my body and the thrust of the oars. My marker light, a candle lantern on a shoreline boulder, throws cat-eyes in the wake until I round the point and it's gone.

Darkness pales around the granite outcrops, gathers heavily in the conifers, looms around the high peaks and opens at the ragged horizon where stars begin. In the darkness of the lake, the deepest black of all, stars swim with an ominous, flat glint. The surface seems less like a mirror than like a window on a galaxy beneath, a fragile membrane between voids. For an instant, there is no up or down. I miss a stroke and the splash leaps up to lick my face with chill.

I should be near the spot, between a cliff and silver snag of dead limber pine. I peer into the dark, ship the oars and drift into sudden quiet. Little, cold feet walk up my back.

I know this place in daylight, having come here to catch this water in bottles, test it for pH and alkalinity, take its temperature and seine it for aquatic insects and plankton. I've carried it out of the mountains, filtered it, preserved it, labeled it and shipped it to far-off labs

194

Dean Krakel

Lake in the Wind River Mountains

where people I've never met subject it to tests: aluminum, calcium, carbon, chlorides, fluorides, iron, lead, magnesium, manganese, ammonium, nitrates, phosphates, potassium, silica, sulfates. I've caught and eaten its trout, scooped it into pots for coffee, mixed it with my blood, taught it to walk and tell lies and pissed it back onto the ground. This lake and I share more than a casual acquaintance, yet in the dark it seems not to know me, to hold me in a blank, star-flecked indifference.

To be unrecognized is, often, to be afraid. So much of human existence is based on recognitions, gestures of belonging: to nations, companies, families, towns, clubs, and classes. Armed with the proper passwords and emblems, we usually go our way in groups and are comforted by it as much as we are oppressed. This nudge of fear creates forms as diverse as herds of elk and political parties. To feel it here and now is natural: it comes with the body and the mind.

No reason to doubt the boat, an Avon inflatable that could float a baby elephant, nor the weather. Apart from mild night breezes, it will stay open and calm under elevated clouds.

I could fear my own error: Li Po, the Old Wine Genius of Chinese poetry, is said to have died when drunk, leaning from a boat to embrace the reflected moon. He fell through the white dazzle and drowned. I have neither wine, nor moon, nor the absolute clumsiness required to fall from a rubber boat on a still lake, yet the feeling of threat is palpable. The boat ceases its drift; for a moment the silence hovers, sheer and inhuman.

I slip a hand into the water's shifting black; cold, but no monster rises and gapes from the deep.

Hello, lake.

Fear is real, though not always accurate. Given the state of the world, there are few places safer then the center of an alpine lake on a fine, dark night. Statistics would prove more danger to an overweight businessman in bed asleep in his new ranchstyle on the San Andreas Fault, particularly if his wife happened to hear about that last conference in Chicago. As he commutes to work on a crowded freeway, dependent on the collective judgment of himself and all others within crashing range, he is closer to death than I am now. There are places in this country where it is dangerous simply to walk the streets and breathe the air. Familiarity with danger carries with it a sort of numb acceptance.

How otherwise might we function in a world complete with megalomaniac politicians and nuclear devices?

Enough of drift and thought. I grope for the Van Dorn bottle and find it, slick, heavy, and efficient. Science. I switch on the flashlight and hold it in my teeth, feeling conspicuous in the night. I set the trigger and lower it, watching the swirl around the white line as it disappears, counting marks until it reaches the proper level. The messenger is a cylindrical brass weight that slips down the rope and bumps the trigger, snapping the ends of the bottle shut. I hear the faint click, haul the loaded bottle and plop it into the raft, then switch the light off. My pupils bloom to admit starlight.

Why am I here? In part because the Forest Service is conducting a study of atmospheric deposition and its effects on these high lakes. The present tests are to assess chemical changes in this lake during a 24-hour period, with tests of pH and alkalinity each four hours. I drew the night shift. Back in camp, where my partner sleeps, are meters and flasks in which water, primed with a chemical indicator, changes color with the measured drip of acid. We record numbers as analogues for the events we observe — abstract-impressionist renderings of the water and its qualities — and arrange them in ways that are significant to scientists, computers, and society. I am a horsepacker and he teaches me hydrology. I teach him good hitches and horse wisdom.

As a working team, we look for omens: clues to this lake's future and, by extension, human fate. We burn no sacred herbs and consult no gods. If I asked a question and an owl called back from the dark, there would be nothing in the message for a computer to gnaw.

We gather data: fragments. From broken shards, archaeologists may infer the sizes and shapes of pots that no longer exist and pose theories to account for their existence, yet a pot can be made only once. A shattered pot becomes something else. It won't hold water.

I listen to the mild slap of water on rubberized fabric. Water is a persistent archetype, the basis of life. Enriched to a warm broth, it surrounds us in the womb. Up here, held in the granite, it is clear, cold, soft, essential. It can be a metaphor for purity: pure as mountain water. Clouds leave it here as snow. Rain races down the rocks and gather before the fall over ledges and talus, a thousand feet down to Gorge Lake, then Suicide Lake, Long Lakes, Fremont Lake, Pine Creek, the New Fork River, the Green, the Colorado, and perhaps the sea, if it has not been evaporated from a reservoir or the cooling towers of a powerplant, has not been claimed for irrigation, thirsty cattle or thirstier cities.

The water itself, universal solvent that it is, does not concern us as much as what it bears: oxides of nitrogen from the autoerotic tangles of the urban West, lead, sulfur compounds from heavy industry, traces of the complex airborne pall that has made hundred-mile views a thing of the past anywhere in the West.

There is no doubt that these waters are tainted — or affected, as a scientist might say. The question is one of degree: Will a certain species of daphnia cease to exist in certain lakes or a pH-sensitive mayfly fail to reproduce? Will the trout die as a result? What are the relative values of brookies in Wyoming and copper-industry jobs in Arizona? How many angels can dance on the head of a pin?

The same question can be asked in terms of values: What are we going to care about and what are we going to do? If we are poisoning our headwaters at the source, then how are we to live? What shall we do with out notions about purity and nature and wilderness? On the other hand, what if the studies, after due argument and interpretation, read "measurable though insignificant degradation of water-resource quality, given present concentrations of airborne acid precursors, for the next 25-year period, assuming no augmentation or spatial redistribution of point-sources or load-levels?" Will this be a signal to reinsert the national head in the national posterior and get back to business as usual?

Perhaps. Scientists swarm in these mountains, taking cores from lakebeds and glaciers, clipping foliage and scraping lichens, carrying bits and pieces back to labs from Maine to California. Conclusions will differ, though it's probably safe to say no one will claim beneficial effects on alpine ecosystems from airborne pollutants.

Strange how quickly thoughts can remove you from a place.

Returning, I feel safe, even loved. The lake and the darkness seem acceptant; clean and perfect in a way I can sense but never grasp. The oars fit smoothly into their locks, but I'm not ready to go; to clamber back onto the rock of the world again to meters and flasks, numbers and names, duties and debts, tents to be folded and horses to catch.

I like this silence in which there is hunger but no greed; such beauty is absolute. I feel the urge that drew Li Po out of the boat to the reflection of the selfless, bright moon, which offered nothing and everything.

The reflection of light on black water has no measurable depth, yet stars wink at me from the lake. This change from fear to calm has come over me many times, but it doesn't take; it will not abide. Any move I make will take me back.

I dip the oars and pull. The boat surges, rounding the invisible, rocky point. The candle in the lantern still burns, warmer and closer than the stars. Among the mirrored stars, a path of dancing light extends across the water, gold as willow leaves, and on it I return.

26

Reworking the Colorado River Basin

Ed Marston

The big structures and diversions are mostly in place on the Colorado River. Hoover Dam backs up 35 million acre-feet in Lake Mead, near Las Vegas, while Lake Powell floods Glen Canyon in Utah with 33 million acre-feet. Smaller dams—Flaming Gorge, Blue Mesa, Navajo—control the Green, the Gunnison and the San Juan. Hundreds of yet smaller dams regulate the tributaries—the North Forks, the South Forks, the Muddies, the Clear Forks . . .

In the lower basin, the water is taken out of the Colorado River via a few very large straws. Southern California diverts its drinking water from Parker Dam just downstream of Hoover, and pumps it westward in the Colorado River Aqueduct. The Imperial and Coachella valley farmers take their one-sixth share of the river out downstream at Imperial Dam and ship it via the All-American Canal to their desert lands. A few large Arizona irrigation districts tap the river after it emerges from the Grand Canyon.

It is different in the upper basin, above Lake Powell. There the Colorado River and its tributaries are nicked by many, many relatively small diversions. A major set of diversions are found along the Continental Divide in Colorado. There, at the river's headwaters, irrigation districts and cities take water out of the Colorado River

basin and send it eastward via tunnels and canals into the Missouri River basin. Water escaping that eastern fate flows downhill to be diverted from the Colorado and its tributaries at thousands of points by farms, towns, cities, and industry.

All together, the upper and lower basin diversions in the late 1970s consumed 11 million acre-feet a year out of a virgin basinwide flow of 14 million acre-feet; three million acre-feet reached Mexico. The 11 million acre-feet were shipped out of the basin, evaporated from reservoirs or taken up by plants.

Although the basin does not have a lot more water to give, three major diversions are in the works: the Central Arizona Project, the Central Utah Project, and a set of collectively large transmountain diversions from the headwaters in Colorado to the Denver Front Range.

The Last Big Ones

When the Central Arizona Project is at full strength in a few years, sending water from behind Parker Dam to Phoenix and Tucson, it will be able to suck two million acre-feet yearly out of the river. Much of it, according to the 1922 Colorado River Compact, belongs to the upper basin states of Colorado, Wyoming, Utah and New Mexico. As those states develop their water over the next 50 years, CAP will cut down its diversion, possibly to as little as 500,000 acre-feet a year.

The Central Utah Project is smaller than CAP. It will take 170,000 acre-feet out of Colorado River basin streams in eastern Utah and transport them west through the mountains for use by farms and cities in the Salt Lake City area. Both CUP and CAP are being built by the Bureau of Reclamation with big federal subsidies. They are part of the government's fulfillment of its promise to help Colorado River states develop their shares of the river.

Colorado has the largest claim to undeveloped water in the Colorado River. It now consumes about two million acre-feet annually out of a share of three million acre-feet. On the Western Slope, with oil shale dead, the only hope for water development is construction of federally subsidized dams.

Such construction, however, does not guarantee use of the water. The Bureau of Reclamation recently completed McPhee Dam on the Dolores River in southwestern Colorado. But many of the farmers who signed up to take the water are desperately trying to escape that obligation. They say it will bankrupt them. Their plight is being used in the fight by environmentalists against the Animas-LaPlata Project, another rural project costing about one half billion dollars, and located near the Dolores Project.

If Colorado does succeed in further dewatering the Colorado River in the near future, it won't be through dams for agriculture and energy. It will rather be through new diversions to the Front Range metro area that stretches from Fort Collins in the north to Colorado Springs and Pueblo in the south. The Front Range cities and farmers already take 500,000 acre-feet a year; additional large and small projects are in the works.

The largest of the several proposed new projects is Two Forks — a 1.2 million acre-foot reservoir on the South Platte River near Denver. It is being sponsored by 46 or so public entities led by Denver. The Front Range has tapped into most of the water close to the Continental Divide. The large capacity of Two Forks wll let the cities penetrate much deeper into western Colorado to bring that water under the Continental Divide for safekeeping on the Front Range itself.

The complexity and scale of the effort is illustrated by the environmental impact statement (EIS) that is examining the Front Range's water options and the permitting of Two Forks and some smaller projects. The EIS has already cost Denver and its partners an extraordinary $35 million — enough to build a small water project even in these inflated times.

That money has loosed on the world an enormous amount of information. But its main result has been to illuminate the structural political problems faced by the Front Range. Denver is a static city of 500,000 barred by law from annexing neighboring land. It is unable to lead the 2.5 million person metropolitan area. Morever, its fellow counties and cities have been unable to come together to create a single entity, such as southern California's Metropolitan Water District, to pursue large, expensive water projects. The metro area's inability to deal collectively with water is symptomatic of similar problems: everything from the sharing of the retail sales tax base to the provision of cultural and health services.

This is a particularly difficult time for the Denver area to be considering an expensive water project. An incredible 30 percent of its offices stand empty. The lack of people in offices and high-tech factories is mirrored in housing. In many neighborhoods, utility poles are festooned with *For Rent* and *For Sale* ads posted by desperate homeowners and landlords. Only Colorado Springs, with its Star Wars industry, thrives.

Discouraged by the gold-plated EIS and the roadblocks in the path of Two Forks, some Colorado cities have begun to poach on Front Range agricultural water, buying up farms and water companies. Even though it means the end of farming for both farmers and their communities, the farmers are going along with the sales, and even seeking them in some cases. The alternative is often foreclosure or bankruptcy.

Salting and Desalting

The quiet issue in the Colorado River basin is salinity. The Colorado River starts out pure at its headwaters, but it naturally picks up a very tolerable 4.7 million tons of salt in its trip to the Gulf of California.

However, that natural saltiness has been aggravated over the years by diversions of pure water out of the headwaters that reduces the water available for dilution. In addition, the use of water for irrigation by farmers and ranchers in the upper basin about doubles the salt load by the time the river reaches the lower Colorado.

The result is a salt concentration at southern California and Mexico diversion points of about 900 parts per million — enough to damage plumbing and industrial fixtures and to stunt crops. It is estimated that each additional part per million of salt causes $600,000 in damage. Put another way, each 11,000 tons of salt added to the river causes $600,000 in damage in the lower basin and Mexico.

Further development in the upper basin, such as new diversions to the Front Range and additional irrigation of salt-laden Wyoming, Utah and Colorado soil, would mean more damage to the lower basin and Mexico. At the same time, given the formal and informal bargains struck among the seven basin states and the federal government, salinity cannot be used to stop water development in the upper basin states.

The result has been a complex, expensive dance. With the Salinity Control Act of 1974, Congress undertook to keep everyone whole. In essence, it pledged to spend what was necessary to control salinity while not hindering upper basin development.

That policy is visible in Colorado's broad, fertile Grand Valley around Grand Junction, near the Utah border. Farmers there use the Colorado River to irrigate 70,000 acres of land. In large part because of the irrigation, the Colorado River picks up an additional 580,000 tons of salt each year in the Grand Valley. The 580,000 tons raises the salinity level in southern California 53 ppm, and causes a theoretical $31 million in damage each year.

To reduce that burden while allowing additional development in the upper basin, the federal government plans to remove 370,000 tons of salt from the river by improving canals, ditches and farming practices.

Of the total, 230,000 tons will be removed by improving on-farm ditches and farming practices. That part is under the control of the Soil Conservation Service. It consists of lining or piping small, seepy dirt ditches, and of encouraging farmers to put just enough water on the ground to nourish the crops without percolating deep into the salty layers of the soil. The total cost will be $35 million, of which the federal government will pay 70 percent and the farmers 30 percent.

The project is noncontroversial. The Soil Conservation Service, a part of the Department of Agriculture, works one-on-one with farmers. Its contract arrangements are simple, it doesn't ask for easements or rights-of-way, and farmers generally feel as though they are getting an improved farm even as they remove salt from the river. A large chunk of the on-farm work is done or underway.

But the 230,000 tons the SCS program will remove isn't enough. So Congress, with some help from hydropower revenues in the upper and lower basins, will spend $250 million more to remove 143,000 tons of salt off-farm. This part of the program consists of lining the big canals that carry water from the Colorado River to the farm areas. It will also be used to line or pipe the medium-sized canals, or off-farm laterals, which carry water from the major canals to groups of farmers.

This program is in the hands of the Interior Department's Bureau of Reclamation, and it is controversial. Some shareholders in the area's largest canal, the Grand Valley Irrigation Company, fear that the Bureau and the state of Colorado are engaging in a land and water grab as part of the salinity control program.

The Bureau entered the program in a heavy-handed way. Unlike the Soil Conservation Service, the Bureau doesn't know how to deal with many small water users. To accommodate its own centralized nature, it insisted that the farmers organize themselves so that it would only have to deal with one entity. Moreover, it wanted that entity to be able to condemn ditch rights-of-way if farmers refused to cooperate voluntarily. The Bureau also created suspicion by demanding that all ditches be lined, even if the farmers had already gotten together to line them. The result has been a revolt among some farmers, a delay in the project and a steady softening of position by the Bureau.

Even had the Bureau and its helper, the state's Colorado Water Conservation Board, been less clumsy initially, there would probably have been suspicion among the many shrewd Grand Valley farmers. Anyone who can do simple arithmetic has got to question the logic of spending $250 million on 70,000 acres of salt-producing land.

The $250 million works out to over $3,000 an acre. If the government were to offer even $2,000 an acre, probably every farmer in that valley would leap to sell. In fact, a large percentage of the land wasn't farmed in 1986. Much of it fell into the hands of speculators and developers during the last oil shale boom, and that, plus depressed farm prices and numerous foreclosures, have led to a lot of land being left fallow.

From a purely market stance, the retirement of the Grand Valley's 70,000 acres from farming, and thus from salt production, makes sense. But such a buy-out would mean the creation of an Owens Valley, of *Chinatown* fame, in western Colorado for the benefit of southern California, Mexico and the urban Front Range. However much economic sense such a step may make, it does not yet make political sense. So the federal government has chosen to spend $250 million to fix the system without making political waves, other than those that come from federal-budget deficits.

The farmers are in an interesting postition. They know their water is very valuable to urban areas. They know their farming causes $31 million a year in downstream damages even as they struggle to survive. Politically, they can't stop the desalting efforts, since the Bureau's program doesn't cost them anything. But they will continue to be very touchy over any attempts by the Bureau to get pushy over rights-of-way and easements.

Even if the farmers keep control of the water, they may be in a worsening position as the Bureau program continues. Thus far, the Bureau has only spent about 20 percent of the $250 million. As it sinks more and more into canal improvement, the Grand Valley land and water will become less and less valuable, since it will be less of a problem to the developing and developed parts of the basin. No one will pay them just to stop them from farming any more.

Kent and Donna Dannen

Grand Valley fields, western Colorado

If irrigated agriculture in the upper basin recovers, then the ditch lining and piping project guarantees Grand Valley farmers a continued existence. But if agriculture is to continue to slide downhill, then the time for Grand Valley farmers to make their Owens Valley deal may be now, while they are still pouring millions of tons of salt a year into the Colorado River.

The Snowpack Reservoir

The headwaters of almost all Western rivers are on national forests. A major reason, perhaps the reason, for national forests and the U.S. Forest Service was to safeguard watersheds. The 1897 Organic Act, the foundation of national forest management, reads:

". . . No national forest shall be established, except to improve and protect the forest within the boundaries, or for the purpose of securing favorable conditions of waterflows, and to furnish a continuous supply of timber for the use and necessities of citizens of the United States. . ."

One would expect to find the agency heavy with hydrologists, fishery biologists and water-quality experts. One would look for policy manuals to bulge with directives on water quality and quantity. In fact, only a small percentage of the agency's employees are specialists in water. And the agency's manual is almost devoid of water-quality policy. Law professor Charles Wilkinson, in a 1985 *Oregon Law Review* article, wrote that the Forest Service has not implemented its authority to control water quality:

"Unfortunately, confusion and misconceptions about the NFMA's (National Forest Management Act) applicability to national forest water-quality issues seem to be pervasive. The Forest Service manual's cursory provisions on water quality may result from a perceived lack of agency authority over water quality. But the NFMA water quality provisions, which are subsequent to and more specific than section 208 of the Clean Water Act 1972, plainly supplement the Clean Water Act requirements for national forest lands."

Wilkinson writes that the approach to water quality has been controversial since the agency tilted away from water and toward timber in the 1940s. The controversy surfaced most loudly in the 1960s' struggle over clearcutting and overcutting on the Monongahela and Bitterroot national forests of West Virginia and Montana/Idaho, leading in 1976 to passage of the NFMA.

Its passage has not settled all battles over water on national forests. The struggle resurfaced recently on the Gunnison National Forest in western Colorado's Delta County. There, a group of farmers south of the Grand Mesa have directed their four small water companies to oppose a plan to build roads to cut several hundred million board-feet of timber over the next 150 years. The first 10 years of the plan will not affect their water, but the farmers fear road construction will set the stage for damaging development.

Their objections persuaded the agency to do an environmental impact statement; now the farmers will appeal the results of the EIS. They have thus far spent about $15,000 fighting the plan, according to Mark Welsh, the consultant-activist the farmers hired to represent them.

The two sides disagree over the economics of the logging, the need for the timber, the effect on wildlife, the need for more roaded recreation, and so on. But the landowners, most of whom have other jobs to support their farms, mainly fear that long-term cutting in the 35,000-acre Stevens Gulch area will alter the flow of water off the hillsides each summer. They catch the flow in hillside-hugging ditches, and convey it to their land by gravity flow. They also fear the alteration will be permanent. The same Paonia Ranger District so intensively logged another high-altitude part of its domain, the Black Mesa, that the forest is not recovering.

The farmers' written objections state that the cutting of trees above their ditches will expose each year's snowpack to stronger sunlight than at present, resulting in earlier runoff. If the ditch companies had reservoirs to catch their water, the timing would not matter. But their reservoir is the snowpack. They depend on slow melting to provide them with water late into the summer. A quick, early melt would deprive them of late summer water.

The Forest Service says its computer model shows that any early melt will be offset by increased moisture in the snowpack caused by the cutting of the trees. The EIS also says that increased sediment due to roading and skidding will not be excessive. Welsh says the agency has done a quick and dirty job of investigating the hydrologic effects, that it has not examined all watersheds the farmers are concerned about, and that its roading program is driven by the availability of money rather than by the resources.

The factual questions are interesting. More interesting is the agency's response to the farmers' repeated requests for a clear policy statement on water in the EIS, and an application of that policy to Stevens Gulch. Their requests were not answered. The draft EIS has a brief discussion of water policy. The final EIS and record of decision by Forest Supervisor Raymond Evans have no policy in them.

Although the agency has chosen not to discuss its policy on water quantity in the EIS, and its application to the specific roading and logging, its policy is clear. One 1986 briefing paper describes the policy as directed at "a range and duration of in-channel flows necessary to maintain the stability and effective function of the streams' channel." Translated, that means the agency seeks a high enough spring flow to clean out sediment that may have accumulated in stream channels. Without such structural flows, channels become filled in and overgrown.

The "structural" water position is a fallback for the agency. Its original position was that it was entitled to reserved water rights to maintain fisheries, recreation and so on, on all national forests. It argued that the Congress, in establishing national forests, also established an implicit federal right to water, just as Indian reservations are entitled to water.

The U.S. Supreme Court in its 1978 Rio Mimbres decision (Rio Mimbres is a river in New Mexico's Gila National Forest) said differently. It ruled that forests' only reserved rights are for stream maintenance and timber. And in the thirsty West, even getting that water has been a struggle. In Colorado, the state and water users are opposing agency attempts in the court to establish such reserved rights. If the states and water interests have their way, the Forest Service will be treated as just another water user.

The Forest Service seems transfixed by Rio Mimbres. Policy

papers and agency officials come back repeatedly to that case. The draft EIS on Stevens Gulch mentioned structural flows. The court's limitation of the agency's pursuit of reserved rights appears to have become its maximum position in all water situations. The farmers protesting the roading and logging plan, for example, are not concerned with agency claims to reserved rights. They want, Welsh says, the Forest Service to control the impacts on water quantity and quality that may be caused by its own timber policy. They want it to put more emphasis on water and less on timber, he says.

Recovering the Squawfish, et al.

Although there are plenty of dams on the upper Colorado River, it is still more river than reservoir. Unlike the lower Colorado, and the Columbia and Missouri, the upper Colorado still looks like a river. But it is an altered river. The dams reduce spring flows, change water temperatures in summer and fall, block fish migration, catch silt, and create and destroy habitat.

One result has been to destroy or endanger four species of fish native to the Colorado: the Colorado squawfish, the humpback chub,

David Sumner

Endangered humpback chub

the bonytail chub, and the razorback sucker. Their plight has not attracted the same attention as the Columbia River's salmon because the Colorado fish have neither sport nor commercial value.

Moreover, the natural river the endangered species are adapted to is one most people do not find attractive: highly variable flows, very warm water at times, lots of silt, and flooding and scouring in springtime.

The Colorado River has been transformed from that early river. Especially in the lower basin, but also in the upper basin, it has been changed into a series of mountain streams, with new "headwaters" starting at each major dam. Large reservoirs reset the river by capturing the silt and the cold runoff in the spring. When the water is released in the summer and fall, it flows from the bottom of the reservoir, clear and cold, as if it were snowmelt coming off the mountains.

The result has been to create "gold medal" conditions for such exotic, or non-native, species as cutthroat trout, rainbow trout, brook trout, and so on. They now thrive in the clear, cold water below Hoover, Flaming Gorge, Blue Mesa, Glen Canyon and other river sections where they once were not found. In addition, catfish, bass, northern pike, and other introduced species find new habitat in the reservoirs.

Some of the introduced species also prey on the native fish. At its full fighting weight of 80 pounds, the squawfish can take care of itself. But its young are easy prey to various introduced species. Moreover, the squawfish is a migratory species — the white salmon of the Colorado — and the dams block it from reaching its breeding places.

The situation appears beyond repair in the lower basin, where the intensity of damming and diversion has wiped out the native fish, and replaced them with introduced varieties. The upper basin has relatively few dams and a relatively low level of diversion, so the native fish are hanging on, for the moment.

For obvious reasons, there has been no support for the squawfish and its endangered brethren from sportsmen, and the water developers have been scornful of these "trash" fish. In fact, the Colorado water establishment attempted to gut the Endangered Species Act in the 1985 Congress to prevent its application to Colorado River dams and diversions. The Endangered Species Act has the potential to block water projects, or to force existing projects to alter the ways in which they operate.

The issue was brought to a head in the early 1980s by a U.S. Fish and Wildlife Service proposal to restore pre-1960s flows to the upper basin. The reaction was intense, and the result was the creation of a coordinating committee to seek a compromise.

The committee was made up of the Fish and Wildlife Service, the Bureau of Reclamation, the states of Colorado, Utah, and Wyoming, the water developers and environmentalists. Surprisingly, the committee hammered out a compromise.

The compromise gives dam builders and water diverters freedom from proving that their particular effect on the river won't further weaken the fish. But it also commits the private developers, the Bureau of Reclamation, and the states to help recover the fish, rather than just prevent further deterioration.

The key to the plan is a $10 million initial appropriation from Congress to purchase water rights to help the fish. Congress will also be asked to appropriate $2.4 million a year for recovery. The kitty will be fattened by a fee each new water development must pay toward the recovery.

The Bureau of Reclamation, whose management of existing dams plays a large role in the regulation of the river, has committed 15,000 acre-feet out of Colorado's Ruedi and Blue Mesa reservoirs. The water will be released at key times to improve the spawning of the native fish species. Funds will also be used to build fish ladders to aid migration, to do biological research (little is now known about the fish), to produce hatchery fish, and to take other steps to improve habitat.

An important role will be played by the states. Colorado, Utah and Wyoming now all have instream flow laws on the books. So the legal means exist to keep water in streams as a beneficial use. Prior to passage of those laws, there was no way to prevent the total dewatering of streams.

The fact that the states, the water developers, and the environmental community have agreed to the recovery program gives it a good chance of obtaining funds from Congress. But there are obstacles. Sport fishing interests fear that the recovery effort will harm trout habitat downstream of dams. And some upper basin interests ask why the lower basin is getting off free. They say California and Arizona are being rewarded for having totally destroyed the native fish and their habitat in the lower Colorado.

27

The Snow Also Rises

Allen Best

In 1983, for reasons of no consequence here, I briefly worked as a snowmaker at the SilverCreek Ski Area. The resort is located on the west flank of the Indian Peaks Wilderness Area, 20-odd miles from where the infant Colorado River flows out of Rocky Mountain National Park in Colorado.

Although snowfall is plentiful in the surrounding mountains, SilverCreek's top elevation is only 9,200 feet and even in January, bushes and rocks occasionally show. That's when I made snow.

Making snow is a simple process, even in the dark. You merely combine water and compressed air at the nozzle of a snowgun. The colder it gets, the less water you need, and the easier it is to make big mounds. The job is no more complicated than irrigating a hay field.

But like irrigating, it does take time. All night we buzzed around on snowmobiles, dragging heavy hoses to the air and water spigots lined along the trails, rassling the heavy snowmaking guns into position, and adjusting and readjusting the mixture of air and water until we were producing just the right kind of snow crystals.

Good man-made snow crystals are unlike the star-shaped flakes that fall naturally. The manufactured variety are small and dense,

A snow-making machine

more like sleet than snow. Man-made snow weighs at least 25 pounds per cubic foot; natural snow in Colorado weighs 12 to 15 pounds.

Ski racers love man-made snow because of its density. When Vail hosts the World Cup races in March, racers ski on man-made snow cranked out for the occasion. Because of the density, it's more durable and the 50th racer encounters virtually the same conditions as the first racer. Natural snow on a race course steadily deteriorates.

The rule of thumb for achieving the preferred crystal is to mix four parts air to one part water. A computer controls the air pressure, but snowmaking is still more art than science, and the quality of the next day's skiing depends on the judgment of someone standing on a dark ski slope, swaddled in layers of clothing, with a miner's lamp on his or her head. Next to him is a snowgun blasting like a powered-up jet plane, which he adjusts depending on how the ice crystals bounce off his glove.

Finally, at dawn, we blew out the hoses, and the snowgroomers took over. I went home to bed, arising in time for the setting sun. If it sounds dull, it was.

Dull or not, snowmaking is vital to SilverCreek and ski resorts around the world. Come November and cold weather, people want to go skiing, with vacations planned months in advance. Opening dates are set months in advance. This tremendous investment is underwritten by snowmaking, the "life insurance policy of ski areas."

Snowmaking became a vital element of the Colorado ski industry relatively late. The basic technology existed in the 1960s, and most New England ski areas invested heavily. But Colorado resorts were slow to follow. Skiing was not yet big business, and it always snowed by January.

That changed during the 1970s. First, the ski industry boomed. With the new automatic-release bindings, people could ski without risking broken bones each time they slid off a lift chair. Along with the better equipment came out-of-state skiers willing to shell out for expensive skiing vacations. At many resorts, destination skiers outnumbered Coloradoans.

In the midst of this boom, Mother Nature brought the industry to its knees. Snow was spare during the 1977-78 season and people across the country stayed away by the planeload.

That winter was viewed as a fluke, but after several more record-setting seasons, Mother Nature failed even more spectacularly in the winter of 1980-81. Trails at Breckenridge and Steamboat were brown at Christmas and they never got much better. The message was clear, and by the next year, virtually every ski hill was putting in air compressors and water pumps.

Today, snowmaking covers a quarter of the ski acreage in Colorado. It enables ski areas across the state to promise that they will open, and it allows some ski areas to guarantee when they will open.

This insurance policy is not cheap. At Vail, it took the first 17,200 skiers last year to pay for snowmaking operating costs. That excludes the over $3 million capital investment. Several years ago, Winter Park figured it cost $16,028 per acre of man-made snow. At SilverCreek, three years ago, the electricity bill dropped from $40,000 a month to $4,000 a month when snowmaking ended.

The effect of snowmaking on water resources of the upper Colorado River drainage is increasingly significant. Ski resorts on the upper Colorado River drainage, from Crested Butte to Steamboat, collectively use nearly 4000 acre-feet, or as much water as is needed for 16,000 people. Most of that water is consumed on the main stem, above Glenwood Canyon. In contrast, according to a study by the industry trade group, Colorado Ski Country U.S.A., 1.5 million acre-feet are used in Colorado for municipal and industrial use in a year; agriculture uses 16 million acre-feet. So on a river basin scale, snowmaking is invisible. But local impacts of snowmaking are already significant and likely to become more significant.

First, snowmaking normally occurs in late fall and early winter, among the driest months of the year. Streams are at their lowest flows, and snowmaking reduces them further. More important, snowmaking is most needed during and after drought years, when there is even less water in headwater streams. And ski resorts, of course, are generally found at the top of river drainages.

The various resorts are dealing with this problem in different ways. Vail is enlarging a small dam near the summit of Vail Pass. Water officials say that this five-fold increase in reservoir storage will allow them to release enough water in drought winters to guarantee a wintertime flow of about six cubic feet per second in Gore Creek even while the snowmaking machines operate full blast. The augmentation scheme promises to accommodate not just snowmaking, but also more condos. A peak population of 40,000 is planned, compared to current peak of 25,000.

Summit County has taken a different approach. It has a peak population of 60,000 and three resorts now with snowmaking: Breckenridge, Copper Mountain, and Keystone. Each of the three areas has signed comprehensive agreements with the Colorado Water Conservation Board, promising to restock streams with fish if, in the event of another drought year, they must drain the waterways below levels at which the fish can survive.

Winter Park, part of the Denver parks system, gets water from the Denver Water Board, which has nearby diversion facilities. Denver doesn't need the water in the winter, and it gets most of the water back when the snow melts in the spring.

But not all ski areas are lucky enough to tie into the Denver Water Board's system, and the demand for winter water has prompted a scheme centered on the Shoshone hydroelectric plant in Glenwood Canyon. That plant has a 1905 water right to a 1250 cubic feet per second, which it sends through its turbines. The scheme calls for satisfying the right by taking the water as it flows out of the plant's discharge pipes and pumping it back upstream to the plant's intake pipes.

The idea, which was hatched by water attorney Scott Balcomb, makes no sense from an energy point of view. It will take about 120 kilowatts of power from another source for Shoshone to produce 100 kilowatts. But endlessly recycling the same water at Shoshone lets upriver ski areas draw the river down below 1250 cfs for snowmaking and other uses. The plan may be moot because of Denver's recent arrangement with Public Service Company, discussed in Chapter 20. But it does show the sorts of things ski areas may have to do to get water.

Actually, water is available for the asking to the ski areas out of Green Mountain Reservoir. But the water is priced at $60 an acre-foot by the Colorado River Water Conservation District, which has been

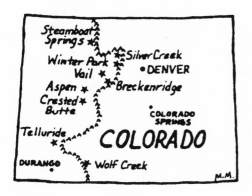

Stars indicate some of Colorado's downhill ski areas. The Continental Divide is shown.

given the water-sale franchise by the Bureau of Reclamation. The ski areas object to the huge profit the River District will make at $60 an acre-foot.

Glenn E. Porzak, an attorney for Vail Associates says: "The actual cost to the River District is $3 to $5 an acre-foot. Green Mountain Reservoir was not put there to give a profit to the middleman, the River District, with which to build future projects. Green Mountain was built for future users on the Western Slope, particularly those upstream of the Shoshone Plant."

Those future users, says Porzak, are now there in the form of ski resorts. Vail, unlike the Summit County resorts, might have initially gone along with the $60 charge if the River District had planned future projects of greater benefit to ski resorts. But now, if Vail can get water for $30 an acre-foot in the Balcomb pump-back scheme, there's no need to spend $60 an acre-foot for Green Mountain water.

"Out future needs will depend upon smaller, strategically placed reservoirs," he says, ones higher up on river drainages. Instead, the River District anticipates a large dam, perhaps on Muddy Creek, just north of Kremmling.

Porzak says the dispute illustrates conflicting attitudes about water use on the upper Colorado River. The big reservoir eyed by the River District would be of use to agricultural interests that are the traditional constituency of the River District, he says. But there is little new demand for agricultural water rights. The demand comes from recreation, now the largest industry on the Western Slope. And the recreation industry, he says, wants small projects, located on headwater streams, to maintain minimum flows through tourist towns and augment streamflows for downriver calls.

Despite the lavish outlays by Colorado ski areas in the last year, evidence is strong that the number of skiers has leveled off. At first glance, that would seem to indicate that these elaborate machinations on the upper Colorado River are unnecessary. But Porzak says that a flat market for skiers will instead increase snowmaking demands.

If you indeed have a flat industry, then to compete for that stable base you must offer a higher quality product, he says, with more high-speed lifts and more snowmaking, to put you one step ahead of your competitor. That, in turn, means higher lift ticket prices.

With Vail already at $35 and other ski resorts on the upper Colorado not far behind, some question how many people can afford to pay for that improved product.

Selected Reading List

Peter Wild

If you are interested in knowing more about the themes of the preceding chapters, the following books are a good place to start. This is a selective, annotated list that emphasizes general river books and books on the Colorado basin.

The Monkey Wrench Gang, by Edward Abbey (Philadelphia: Lippincott, 1975). This novel has dams rising sky-high and high-speed chases as a band of eco-raiders attempts to right technology's wrongs with dynamite. An excursion through environmentalists' wish fulfillment.

The Gila: River of the Southwest, by Edwin Corle (New York: Rinehart, 1951). This book deals with a tributary, but it is a key to the variety of the immense watershed drained by the Colorado. It covers the Spanish conquest and the folklore, flora, and fauna of a subregion's "burning deserts and snow-capped mountains."

Across the Wide Missouri, by Bernard DeVoto (Boston: Houghton Mifflin, 1947). An account of the early fur trade in the Rocky Mountains that further confirms the early economic importance of rivers.

The Journals of Lewis and Clark, by Bernard DeVoto (Boston: Houghton Mifflin, 1953). One of the best introductions to the early nineteenth-century stage of westering. Lewis and Clark's journeys demonstrated the advantage of the West's watercourses, disconnected as they might be, as highways for later exploitation and settlement.

Water Scarcity: Impacts on Western Agriculture, edited by Ernest A. Englebert (Berkeley: University of California Press, 1984). A reflection of the latest decade's realization that the West's often-failing rivers are barometers of the region's general health. The volume gathers a wide number of views on the legal, environmental, and economic implications of future water use.

Despite the diversity of the essays, they point to one conclusion: The West's survival will depend on adjustment to a limited resource.

The Chosen Valley, by Mary Hallock Foote (Boston: Houghton Mifflin, 1892). A novel of men struggling beyond their financial and emotional limits to irrigate arid Idaho. The author's misgivings are that "victory, if it come, shall border hard upon defeat."

A River No More, by Philip L. Fradkin (New York: Alfred A Knopf, 1981). Hands down the best place to start reading about the Colorado River. Fradkin pauses on his river journey to fill the reader in on the faulty economics and social patterns generated by the conquest of a once grand resource.

The Central Gold Region: The Grain, Pastoral, and Gold Regions of North America, by William Gilpin (Philadelphia: Sower, Barnes, 1860). In this book's era, an aura of stardust glittered over the West. The fact that much of this vast domain lacked water didn't deter the dreamers. The author, also the first territorial governor of Colorado, calls newcomers West, promising them that there, rain follows the plow and that farmers can take their ease on their front porches while their untended fields of corn and melons grow with abandon.

Overland Journey, by Horace Greeley (New York: C.M. Saxton, Barker, 1860). The New York *Tribune's* eccentric editor's account of his 1859 stagecoach ride across the West to investigate the prospect for farmers. Cautiously optimistic about some of the better-watered valleys, he bluntly described other areas as places where "famine sits enthroned."

Dividing the Waters: A Century of Controversy Between the United States and Mexico, by Norris Hundley (Berkeley: University of California Press, 1966). This scholarly book shows that divvying up the Colorado has had international repercussions. The tug-of-war over the river's overallocated waters has produced chronic sores, not only among the states but between two countries.

Water and the West: The Colorado River Compact and the Politics of Water in the American West, by Norris Hundley (Berkeley: University of California Press, 1975). A documentation of the political circus over converting rivers into dollars with an only tentative perception of the dire consequences.

Reclaiming the Arid West: The Story of the United States Reclamation Service, by George Wharton James (New York: Dodd, Mead, 1917). This is heady literature, typical of its time, proclaiming a "new day" of prosperity based on turning the West's few rivers out of their channels and into farmers' fields.

Muddy Water: The Army Engineers and the Nation's Rivers, by Arthur Maass (Cambridge, Mass.: Harvard University Press, 1951). One of a number of studies throwing doubts on the whole massive manipulation of the West's rivers.

Irrigation: Its Evils, the Remedies and the Compensations, by George Perkins Marsh (Washington, D.C.: 43rd Congress, 1st Session, Senate Misc. Doc. 55, 1874); *Man and Nature,* by George Perkins Marsh (New York: Charles Scribner, 1864). Two warnings that nature could go haywire if meddled with. *Man and Nature* is a massive work, the first scientific account pegging environmental degradation to man's abuses.

Values and Choices in the Development of the Colorado River Basin, edited by Dean F. Peterson and A. Barry Crawford (Tucson: University of Arizona Press, 1978). A compilation of fifteen articles discussing the agricultural, recreational, legal, and other Gordian knots of tangled Colorado controversies. Of special note is Helen Ingram's "Politics of Water Allocation" (pages 61–75). She suggests that the early dreams of water abundance in the arid lands often have turned out to be expensive mirages.

The Place No One Knew, photographs by Eliot Porter (San Francisco: Sierra Club, 1963). This portfolio stung the nation's conscience over the mysteries lost when Glen Canyon Dam inundated a priceless section of the Colorado in 1963. In his introductory essay, David Brower states the obverse of Woodbury's ethic: "The menace is . . . the notion that growth and progress are the same, and that the gross national product is the measure of the good life."

Exploration of the Colorado River of the West and its Tributaries, by John Wesley Powell (Washington, D.C.: U.S. Government Printing Office, 1875). Powell became famous overnight when he shot out of the downstream end of the feared Grand Canyon as its first successful navigator. He penned this book with an eye on Congress and increased aid for further expeditions. It is doubly notable – dramatically, for its day-by-day account of his "impossible" journey, and historically, for its sympathy toward a hostile environment.

Report on the Lands of the Arid Region of the United States, by John Wesley Powell (Washington, D.C.: U.S. Government Printing Office, 1878). In this report, Powell called the attention of Congress to a hard truth: The region's few rivers couldn't possibly create the lush Garden of the West that both officialdom and common wisdom envisioned. Eyebrows were raised at such a lack of patriotism. Booming railroad and real-estate interests branded Powell a heretic and a socialist.

Beyond the Hundredth Meridian: John Wesley Powell and the Second Opening of the West, by Wallace Stegner (Boston: Houghton Mifflin, 1954). Essential, and stylistically gracious, reading for understanding the role of water in shaping the West. Stegner illuminates Powell as the John the Baptist of water reform – the man who battled popular delusions about water abundance in an arid land.

This Is Dinosaur, by Wallace Stegner (New York: Alfred A. Knopf, 1955). This is one of the sacred tales of conservation. In the 1950s, the Bureau of Reclamation decided to build Echo Park Dam on the Green River (actually the main branch of the Colorado). This would flood parts of Dinosaur National

Monument. Heated by the imminent invasion, the grand old men of modern conservation — Stegner, Bernard DeVoto, David Brower, and Howard Zahniser — rallied the nation to preserve Dinosaur's supposedly inviolate treasure. The colorful *This Is Dinosaur* initiated a rallying cry that was later taken up by large-format books on other conservation issues.

War for the Colorado River, by John Upton Terrell (Glendale, Calif.: A.H. Clark, 1965). A two-volume set recounting the legal battles over the Colorado. One supporter of the multimillion-dollar Central Arizona Project raged that without the project, taxes would go up, schools would close, and crime would run rampant through the streets of the Southwest, thus illustrating that hysteria often carried the day.

The Great Plains, by Walter Prescott Webb (Boston: Ginn and Co., 1931). Webb has little to say directly about rivers, but his observations on pioneers' struggles over water and the resulting shifts in law and society showed that the West was shaped by factors far different from dreams.

The Colorado Conquest, by David Oakes Woodbury (New York, Dodd, Mead, 1941). Heroic stories about the taming of what the author calls the menacing "Red Bull," the Colorado. Especially readable is the account of how men got more than they bargained for in 1905, when the "Red Bull" leaped out of its bed, shot down an irrigation ditch, and began flooding California's Imperial Valley. About the successful efforts to put a ring in the river's nose, the author concludes, "The Colorado has met its match at last." An ironic book in light of current events.

Rivers of Empire: Water, Aridity, and the Growth of the American West, by Donald Worster (New York: Pantheon Books, 1985). Worster draws together history, folklore, politics, and economics into a comprehensive overview of the region's rivers. A scholarly but readable achievement, *Rivers of Empire* belongs on the shelf with the handful of books essential to understanding the West.

Run, River, Run, by Ann Zwinger (New York: Harper & Row, 1975). More impressionistic than Philip Fradkin's work mentioned above, this book exemplifies the poetic approach to river-trip books: "Running whitewater is like riding a horse: if you fall off, you'd better get right back on." As is usual in Zwinger's volumes, her graceful drawings parallel a graceful text.

Index

ALSO AVAILABLE
FROM ISLAND PRESS

Land and Resource Planning in the National Forests
By Charles Wilkinson and H. Michael Anderson

Controversy and conflict have marked the debate about the future of our national forests. Originally published as a special issue of the *Oregon Law Review, Land and Resource Planning in the National Forests* has become *the* standard reference source in the field for understanding and analysis of the National Forest Management Act of 1976—the basis for the current forest planning procedures in all of the national forests. Here is a comprehensive tool—an in-depth review and analysis of planning, policy, and law in the national forest system. This book is nontechnical and emphasizes the historical background to the current legislation. Charles Wilkinson is Professor of Law at the University of Colorado Law School. H. Michael Anderson works with The Wilderness Society.

1987. x, 408 pp., index.
Paper, ISBN 0-933280-38-6. **$14.95**

Last Stand of the Red Spruce
By Robert A. Mello; sponsored by National Resources Defense Council

Acid rain—the debates rage between those who believe that the cause of the problem is clear and identifiable and those who believe that the evidence is inconclusive. In *Last Stand of the Red Spruce,* Robert A. Mello has written an ecological detective story that unravels this confusion and explains how air pollution is killing our nation's forests. Writing for a lay audience, the author traces the efforts of scientists trying to solve the mystery of the dying red spruce trees on Camels Hump in Vermont. Mello clearly and succinctly presents both sides of an issue on which even the scientific community is split and concludes that the scientific evidence uncovered on Camels Hump elevates the issues of air pollution and acid rain to new levels of national significance.

1987. xx, 156 pp., illus., references, bibliography.
Paper, ISBN 0-933280-37-8. **$14.95**

The Report of the President's Commission on Americans Outdoors: The Legacy, The Challenge
With Case Studies
Preface by William K. Reilly

"If there is an example of pulling victory from the jaws of disaster, this report is it. The Commission did more than anyone expected, especially the administration. It gave Americans something serious to think about if we are to begin saving our natural resources."—Paul C. Pritchard, President, National Parks and Conservation Association.

This report is the first comprehensive attempt to examine the impact of a changing American society and its recreation habits since the work of the Outdoor Recreation Resource Review Commission, chaired by Laurence Rockefeller in 1962. The President's Commission took more than two years to complete its study; the Report contains over sixty recommendations, such as the preservation of a nationwide network of "greenways" for recreational purposes and the establishment of an annual $1 billion trust fund to finance the protection and preservation of our recreational resources. The Island Press edition provides the full text of the report, much of the additional material compiled by the Commission, and twelve selected case studies.

1987. xvi, 426 pp., illus., appendixes, case studies.
Paper, ISBN 0-933280-36-X.   **$24.95**

Public Opinion Polling: A Handbook for Public Interest and Citizen Advocacy Groups
By Celinda C. Lake, with Pat Callbeck Harper

"Lake has taken the complex science of polling and written a very usable 'how-to' book. I would recommend this book to both candidates and organizations interested in professional, low-budget, in-house polling."—Stephanie Solien, Executive Director, Women's Campaign Fund.

Public Opinion Polling is the first book to provide practical information on planning, conducting, and analyzing public opinion polls as well as guidelines for interpreting polls conducted by others. It is a book for anyone—candidates, state and local officials, community organizations, church groups, labor organizations, public policy research centers, and coalitions focusing on specific economic issues—interested in measuring public opinion.

1987. x, 166 pp., tables, bibliography, appendix, index.
Paper, ISBN 0-933280-32-7.   **$19.95**
Companion software soon to become available.

Green Fields Forever: The Conservation Tillage Revolution in America
By Charles E. Little

"*Green Fields Forever* is a fascinating and lively account of one of the most important technological developments in American agriculture. . . . Be prepared to enjoy an exceptionally well-told tale, full of stubborn inventors, forgotten pioneers, enterprising farmers—and no small amount of controversy."—Ken Cook, World Wildlife Fund and The Conservation Foundation.

Here is the book that will change the way Americans think about agriculture. It is the story of "conservation tillage"—a new way to grow food that, for the first time, works *with,* rather than against, the soil. Farmers who are revolutionizing the course of American agriculture explain here how conservation tillage works. Some environmentalists think there are problems with the methods, however; author Charles E. Little demonstrates that on this issue both sides have a case, and the jury is still out.

1987. 189 pp., illus., appendixes, index, bibliography.
Cloth, ISBN 0-933280-35-1. **$24.95**
Paper, ISBN 0-933280-34-3. **$14.95**

Federal Lands: A Guide to Planning, Management, and State Revenues
By Sally K. Fairfax and Carolyn E. Yale

"An invaluable tool for state land managers. Here, in summary, is everything that one needs to know about federal resource management policies."—Rowena Rogers, President, Colorado State Board of Land Commissioners.

Federal Lands is the first book to introduce and analyze in one accessible volume the diverse programs for developing resources on federal lands. Offshore and onshore oil and gas leasing, coal and geothermal leasing, timber sales, grazing permits, and all other programs that share receipts and revenues with states and localities are considered in the context of their common historical evolution as well as in the specific context of current issues and policy debates.

1987. xx, 252 pp., charts, maps, bibliography, index.
Paper, ISBN 0-933280-33-5. **$24.95**

Hazardous Waste Management: Reducing the Risk
By Benjamin A. Goldman, James A. Hulme, and Cameron Johnson for the Council on Economic Priorities

Hazardous Waste Management: Reducing the Risk is a comprehensive source-book of facts and strategies that provides the analytic tools needed by policy makers, regulating agencies, hazardous waste generators, and host communities to compare facilities on the basis of site, management, and technology. The Council on Economic Priorities' innovative ranking system applies to real-world, site-specific evaluations, establishes a consistent protocol for multiple applications, assesses relative benefits and risks, and evaluates and ranks ten active facilities and eight leading commercial management corporations.

1986. xx, 316 pp., notes, tables, glossary, index.
Cloth, ISBN 0-933280-30-0. **$64.95**
Paper, ISBN 0-933280-31-9. **$34.95**

An Environmental Agenda for the Future
By Leaders of America's Foremost Environmental Organizations

". . . a substantive book addressing the most serious questions about the future of our resources."—John Chaffee, U.S. Senator, Environmental and Public Works Committee. "While I am not in agreement with many of the positions the authors take, I believe this book can be the basis for constructive dialogue with industry representatives seeking solutions to environmental problems."—Louis Fernandez, Chairman of the Board, Monsanto Corporation.

The chief executive officers of the ten major environmental and conservation organizations launched a joint venture to examine goals that the environmental movement should pursue now and into the twenty-first century. This book presents policy recommendations for implementing changes needed to bring about a healthier, safer world. Topics discussed include nuclear issues, human population growth, energy strategies, toxic waste and pollution control, and urban environments.

1985. viii, 155 pp., bibliography.
Paper, ISBN 0-933280-29-7. **$7.95**

Water in the West
By Western Network

Water in the West is an essential reference tool for water managers, public officials, farmers, attorneys, industry officials, and students and professors attempting to understand the competing pressures on our most important natural resource: water. Here is an in-depth analysis of the effects of energy development, Indian rights, and urban growth on other water users.

1985. *Vol. III: Western Water Flows to the Cities*
v, 217 pp., maps, table of cases, documents, bibliography, index.
Paper, ISBN 0-933280-28-9. **$25.00**

Community Open Spaces
By Mark Francis, Lisa Cashdan, and Lynn Paxson

Over the past decade, thousands of community gardens and parks have been developed on vacant neighborhood land in America's major cities. *Community Open Spaces* documents this movement in the United States and Europe, explaining how planners, public officials, and local residents can work in their own communities to successfully develop open space.

1984. xiv, 250 pp., key contacts: resource organizations, appendixes, bibliography, index.
Cloth, ISBN 0-933280-27-0. **$24.95**

Land-Saving Action
Edited by Russell L. Brenneman and Sarah M. Bates

Land-Saving Action is the definitive guide for conservation practitioners. It is a written symposium by the twenty-nine leading experts in land conservation.

This book presents, in detail, land-saving tools and techniques that have been perfected by individuals and organizations across the nation. This is the first time such information has been available in one volume.

1984. xvi, 249 pp., tables, notes, author
bibliographies, selected readings, index.
Cloth, ISBN 0-933280-23-8. **$39.95**
Paper, ISBN 0-933280-22-X. **$24.95**

The Conservation Easement in California
By Thomas S. Barrett and Putnam Livermore for The Trust for Public Land

This is the authoritative legal handbook on conservation easements. *The Conservation Easement in California* examines the California law as a model for the nation, emphasizing the effectiveness and flexibility of the California code. Also covered are the historical and legal backgrounds of easement technology, state and federal tax implications, and solutions to the most difficult drafting problems.

1983. xiv, 173 pp., appendixes, notes, selected bibliography, index.
Cloth, ISBN 0-933280-20-3. **$34.95**

Private Options: Tools and Concepts for Land Conservation
By Montana Land Reliance and Land Trust Exchange

Techniques and strategies for saving the family farm are presented by thirty experts. *Private Options* details the proceedings of a national conference and brings together, for the first time, the experience and advice of land conservation experts from all over the nation.

1982. xiv, 292 pp., key contacts: resources for local conservation organizations, conference participants, bibliography, index.
Paper, ISBN 0-933280-15-7. **$25.00**

These titles are available directly from Island Press, Box 7, Covelo, CA 95428. Please enclose $2.75 shipping and handling for the first book and $1.25 for each additional book. California and Washington, DC residents add 6% sales tax. A catalogue of current and forthcoming titles is available free of charge.

Island Press
Board of Directors